Brands

Brands are now a dominant feature of contemporary living. Drawing on rich empirical material, this book builds up a critical theory, arguing that brands have become an important tool for transforming everyday life into economic value.

Corporate logos are inscribed in our everyday life as companies try to brand a particular life-style or value complex onto their products, working on the assumption that consumers desire products for their ability to give meaning to their lives. However, brands also have a key function within managerial strategy. Examining the history of audience and market research, marketing thought and advertising strategy, Arvidsson traces the historical development of branding. Through his evaluation of new media, contemporary management and overall media economics, he presents a systematic and comprehensive theory of brands.

Brands uses illustrative case studies throughout from market research, advertising, shop displays, mobile phones, the internet and virtual companies. This book will be essential reading for students and researchers in sociology of media, cultural studies, advertising and consumer studies, and marketing.

Adam Arvidsson is Assistant Professor in the Department of Film and Media Studies at the University of Copenhagen. His research examines the economic role of brands within the contemporary information economy.

Brands

Meaning and value in media culture

Adam Arvidsson

LONDON AND NEW YORK

First published 2006
by Routledge
2 Park Square, Milton Park, Abingdon, Oxon OX14 4RN

Simultaneously published in the USA and Canada
by Routledge
270 Madison Ave, New York, NY 10016

Routledge is an imprint of the Taylor & Francis Group

© 2006 Adam Arvidsson

Typeset in Sabon by Book Now Ltd
Printed and bound in Great Britain by
TJ International Ltd, Padstow, Cornwall

All rights reserved. No part of this book may be reprinted or reproduced or
utilized in any form or by any electronic, mechanical, or other means, now
known or hereafter invented, including photocopying and recording, or in
any information storage or retrieval system, without permission in writing
from the publishers.

British Library Cataloguing in Publication Data
A catalogue record for this book is available from the British Library

Library of Congress Cataloging in Publication Data
A catalog record for this book has been requested

ISBN10: 0–415–34715–7 (hbk)
ISBN10: 0–415–34716–5 (pbk)

ISBN13: 9–78–0–415–34715–0 (hbk)
ISBN13: 9–78–0–415–34716–7 (pbk)

Contents

Preface

This book wants to make a very simple argument: that brands should be understood as an institutional embodiment of the logic of a new form of informational capital – much like the factory embodied the logic of industrial capital. Brand management is a matter of putting to work the capacity of consumers (and increasingly other kinds of actors) to produce a common social world through autonomous processes of communication and interaction. This capacity to produce a common social world is empowered and programmed to unfold in ways that create the measurable kinds of attention and affect that underpin the commercial values of brands. Like informational capital in general, brands extract value by putting to work the very basic human capacity to create a common social world. This book thus attempts an analysis of the brand as an institution, and I have tried to capture its logic. There are of course many other things to be said about brands: their role in the life of consumers, their very particular ontological status, how to manage and nurture them, how they can be more or less successful, and so on. This book touches these matters only superficially (but there is a lengthy bibliography). Let me stress from the start that, even though I argue that brands 'work with' or presuppose the 'resistance' or 'agency' of consumers, I do not believe that the control that brand management exercises is 'total' or impossible to escape. On the contrary, by way of a conclusion I argue that the institution of the brand is a symptom of the general weakness of capitalist command that marks informational capitalism. My purpose in this book has been to provide an analysis rather than a critique of brands. To be critical of brands *per se* is about as fruitful as it is to be critical of factories or bureaucracies. Brands are an institution that can be put to good uses as well as bad ones, that can be progressive as well as reactionary. And, I think, brands will be with us for a long time. Today they are mostly used for marketing purposes. But I would not be surprised if the next wave of social movements were to be somehow modelled on the brand, much like the workers movements of the last turn of the century were modelled on bureaucracy.

San Gimignano, 30 July 2005

Acknowledgements

Many people have helped me to write this book. None of them have any responsibility for the shortcomings of the end product. My research builds in part on interviews and participatory observations in the Copenhagen advertising, branding and new media business. I thank everybody who has invited me to workshops and seminars and taken time to talk to me. It developed in discussions with graduate students in Copenhagen, Milan, Siena and Stockholm and as the argument matured it benefited from suggestions and critique from friends and colleagues. I would particularly like to thank Soren Askegaard, Anders Bengtson, Janet Borgeson, John Brewer, Benedetta Cappellini, Egeria di Nallo, Karin Ekström, Alexandra George, Pierre Guillet de Monthoux, Casper Hoegenhaven, Francesco Lapenta, Massimo Leone, Christian Maravelias, Enrico Menduni, Dalia Muktar-Landgren, Pierluigi Musarò, Jonathan Morris, Celia Lury, Per Östergaard, Nikolaj Peitersen and the friends at Kesera, Anders Ramsay, Roberta Sassatelli, Jonathan Schroeder, Don Slater, Krittwatt Wattanasuwan and Magnus Wennerhag. George Ritzer and the anonymous reviewers for the *Journal of Consumer Culture* provided a lot of valuable feedback. Frank Trentman hosted me as a Fellow in the Cultures of Consumption programme at Birkbeck College, London. This gave me the necessary breathing space to finish the book. Finally, this book is dedicated to my friends and discussants, Jon-Erik Lundberg and Filip Josephson, Sweden's foremost expert.

1 Introduction

I'm wearing a lamb's wool topcoat, a wool
jacket with wool flannel trousers, a cotton
shirt, a cashmere V-neck sweater and a silk
tie, all from Armani. Evelyn's wearing a
cotton blouse by Dolce & Gabbana, suede
shoes by Yves Saint Laurent, a stencilled calf
skirt by Adrienne Landau with a suede belt
by Jill Stuart, Calvin Klein tights, Venetian
glass earrings by Frances Patiky Stein, and
clasped in her hand is a single white rose
that I bought at a Korean deli before Carruthers'
limousine picked me up. Carruthers is
wearing a lamb's wool sport coat, a
cashmere/vicuña cardigan sweater, cavalry twill
trousers, a cotton shirt and a silk tie, all from
Hèrmes. ('How tacky', Evelyn whispered to me;
I silently agreed.)

> (Bret Easton Ellis, *American Psycho*,
> New York; Vintage Books, 1991, p. 143)

I am an international student in Canada. I don't have much in my room,
besides an eMac sitting on my desk, and, this is just enough. My eMac is
the only furniture and decoration I need in my room. I spend most of my
time on my eMac to study and get connected with my friendsu [sic] back
home. When the girls come into my room, the first thing they usually
say is: 'wow, you use Apple?', and they automatically assume that I am a
very cool guy that has great taste, and things just get better and better . . .
Thank you, my eMac, for making my life so much more colorful and
exciting!

> (Chi, Canada, testimonial on 'lovemarks', 31 October, 2004)[1]

> I realized the other night that, with perhaps one or two exceptions, every
> guy that I've ever slept with and/or dated has been a total Apple fetishist.
> They all have iBooks (or sometimes PowerBooks), and iPods, and they
> use iTunes and iChat and iPhoto, and sometimes have been known to
> take trips to the famously sexy Apple Store in Soho. It's not unusual for
> me to find myself in a bedroom conversation about why Macs are just so
> much better.
>
> (Missmimesis, The Nerve Blog-a-log entry 29 January, 2005)

Bret Easton Ellis' dystopian account of life among New York yuppies in
the 1980s was arguably the first literary text where brand names played a
prominent part. Ellis' characters are defined by the branded items that
they wear, use or otherwise endow themselves with, and the presence of
one brand instead of another is often what defines a person or triggers a
social situation. Throughout the novel, people remain anonymous and
distant; brands speak for them, define them and make them into what
they are. (And the main character, Patrick Bateman is often taken for a
'Marcus Halberstam', who allegedly wears the same kind of Brooks
Brothers non-prescription glasses.)

  Ellis' novel depicts a period in which the brand in its present form made
its entry on the social scene. In the United States, yuppies, a relatively
small but culturally significant elite, had cast off the last remains of the
progressive heritage of the 1960s and 1970s, to devote themselves to
consumption in the pursuit of life-style and self-realization (Bonner and
du Gay, 1992; Ehrenreich, 1990; Featherstone, 1991). In marketing
brand management became the new paradigm, and advertising went
through its second 'creative revolution' to put a renewed focus on the
construction of image (Mort, 1996; Nixon, 1996, 2003; cf. Seguela,
1982). In the 1980s, the present wave of brand extensions began, building on new possibilities to out-source production. A number of luxury
brands like Armani and Polo Ralph Lauren added on a wide range of new
products – like soap, perfume, home appliances and, in the case of Ralph
Lauren, paint – to end up selling paraphernalia for a more or less
complete life-style (Twitchell, 1996). Some of these, like Pierre Cardin,
over-extended themselves, effectively devaluing the brand name. Logos
acquired a new visibility, and knowledge about brands, what they
signified and how they differed became a central component of the
middle class habitus. Significantly, the rise of brands did not only affect
consumer culture; the world of work was also taken in. In the 1980s,
management discovered the importance of 'organizational identity'
(later 'organizational branding') as a way to give direction and coherence

to complex, transnational organizations, too flexible and adaptive for the old bureaucratic style of command (Heelas, 2002). It now became important to 'sell' the organization, its values and goals to employees, to make them embrace its culture and make it their own (du Gay, 1996; Olins, 2000). Finally, the 1980s saw the efforts of the Reagan administration to privatize and de-regulate media, public space and public institutions. This facilitated the contemporary omnipresence of brands in schools, art museums and across the lived cityscape in general. It also enabled the media mergers and acquisitions that by now have produced the common media culture that makes global branding feasible (Mattelart, 1991; McChesney, 1999).

Although brands have a long history as a commercial institution, reaching as far back as the eighteenth century (see Chapter 5), their position as central components of the social fabric was established in the 1980s. Brands now became something of an omnipresent tool by means of which identity, social relations and shared experiences (like spending a night in bed talking about Apple products) could be constructed. They were spun into the social fabric as a ubiquitous medium for the construction of a common social world.

During the twenty years or so that have passed since the New York of Pat Bateman (when *Les Miserables* were still hot and people carried huge cell phones in their briefcases), much has happened on this front. Advertising budgets have grown steadily (apart from a slight setback in the early 1990s). The branding of public space has accelerated with corporate sponsorship replacing state subsidies for a wide range of institutions within education and the arts. 'Liberalization' of national media markets, combined with new, or more widely accessible technologies like VCRs, cable, satellite, home computers and the internet have made possible a commercial media culture capable of reaching into, appropriating and recycling styles and influences from areas that used to lie beyond the frontiers of consumer culture, such as China, Africa, India and the countries of the former Eastern Bloc, integrating them into a 'commercial ecumene' of well-nigh global dimensions (Fuglesang, 1994; Davies ed., 2000; Rajagopal, 1999; Appadurai, 1996; Hannerz, 1996). Enabled by this world-wide opening up to consumer culture, new brands like Nike and Starbucks have emerged with a global focus, and old one's like McDonald's and Tesco have re-oriented their strategic focus to expand into the new markets of Asia, South America and the Middle East. Many of these global companies now make systematic use of their brands to manage their transnational organizations. Regardless of whether you work at Starbucks in New York, Istanbul or Bangkok, you are part of the same organizational culture, ideally sharing the same values, beliefs and strategies of personal self-presentation. (Generally this does not include the people employed in the out-sourced production of the material goods sold, like the under-paid US prison labour that manufactures Starbucks' disposable paper cups.) Brands have established themselves as an important managerial tool that gives stability and coherence to the Globally Integrated Networks that structure the flows of today's transnational economy (Urry, 2003; Franklin *et al.*, 2000; Lury, 2004).

At the same time, brands have become part of a global popular culture. The kind of knowledgeable, almost obsessive relation to brands that Ellis described among New York yuppies now seems to be extended to a wide range of different consumer groups. Among the Asian middle classes, for example brands have acquired a new importance: 'Not so long ago China's new rich left brand labels attached to the sleeve of their suit jackets, and their newly acquired Rolexes meant that fashion was to have your sleeves rolled up' (French, 1998). Today, effigies of brands like Mercedes and Nokia are sometimes replacing the traditional paper money to be burnt at Chinese funerals. In Malaysia, rich young people form 'Harley Davidson tribes' (Talid, 2000). In the Philippines, less affluent lower middle class youth 'spend hours sitting in strategic places, where they could be seen by all at McDonald's or at Pizza Hut, drinking Coke or Milkshakes with a burger. They would then take the empty hamburger bags with them as they left the fast food restaurant, so that everybody in the street could see where they had their lunch or dinner. Students would share one Benetton sweater with two or three others' (Gerke, 2000). In Bangkok, students from the countryside use strategies of 'symbolic consumption' mediated by brands to accommodate to the urban environment, and their richer peers deploy branded goods to flexibly adapt their self-presentations to the demands of the particular social situation, as they navigate between peer culture, parental expectations and professional life (Wattanasuwan, 2002a, 2002b).

It is true that people have commonly used consumption to mark off their transition from rural to urban environments, from a culture of relative deprivation to one of relative affluence. Italian sociologists Francesco Alberoni and Guido Baglioni's 1965 study of migrants from the Italian South to the industrialized North is a classic in this respect. They showed how migrants viewed refrigerators, cars, washing machines, cosmetics and processed foods not just as conveniences but as tokens of belonging to an urban modernity to which they aspired. But it seems that today's upwardly mobile Asian consumers are different. For them it is not the products as much as the *brands* that matter. Not so much the Hamburger as the McDonald's Hamburger, not so much the watch as the Rolex watch, not so much the stylish handbag as the Prada handbag. It is the significance of the brand, itself articulated in a complex web of commercial intertextuality, that becomes the main use-value of the product: it allows a process positioning, or 'negotiation' of the self in relation to the shifting demands of everyday life. A similar importance of brands in the performance of selfhood and social relations has been noted among American high-school teenagers, particularly those who lack other qualities like athletic prowess or exceptional beauty. To the 'slightly awkward', the 'overweight or not conventionally pretty', savvy display of brands becomes a way of constructing a social position and a passable image (Quart, 2003: 31). While the branded teenage world that Quart describes can be taken as an extreme example, ordinary middle class Americans also take brands seriously. Recent research has shown how people engage in 'brand communities'. They communicate (often over the internet), socialize and create shared friendships and animosities around brands like Saab and Macintosh (Muniz and O'Guinn, 2001). Overall, recent consumer research has come to emphasize that brands – and not just products – are important 'cultural resources' that people relate to as significant components of their own identities and overall life world (Elliott and Wattanasuwan, 1998; Fourier, 1998; Holt, 2002). Some go as far as to claim that, at least in the United States, brands now provide a source of meaning and 'community' capable of replacing those supposedly lost in the modernization process. People may 'bowl alone', but they socialize around brands (Muniz and O'Guinn, 2001; Firat and Venkatesh, 1995; cf. Putnam, 2000). Brands are part of the mundane context of action within which we become subjects.

But this new importance of brands to social life is only one part of the equation. The other part, frequently neglected by academic marketing, popular branding discourse and cultural studies alike, is economic. Parallel to the rise of the brand as a social institution – as something that mediates social life – there has been a clear increase in the financial significance of brand values. Since the 1980s the number of companies capitalizing on their brands have increased, and brand value has acquired a growing weight in financial decisions (Goodchild and Callow, 2001; Wild and Scicluna, 1997). While it is difficult to give exact figures for this development, estimates claim that during the mergers and acquisitions wave of the 1980s about 20 per cent of most bid prices were motivated by the value of brands. During the dot.com boom of the mid-1990s that figure was closer to 70 per cent in some sectors.

Comprehensively Jan Lindemann (2003) of the Interbrand consultancy group estimates that the economic weight of tangible assets in non-financial businesses has decreased from slightly over 70 per cent in 1980 to slightly over 50 per cent in 2000. The corresponding increase in intangible assets includes things like patents and intellectual property rights, but since the relative weight of brands versus other intangibles has increased in the same period a substantial share of this increase is attributable to the growing economic weight of brand values. In parallel to this, there has been a movement in trademark legislation towards a recognition of the brand, not only as a symbol of something else – the quality of a product or the identity of the producer – but as an object of property in its own right. Lury calls this a movement from a definition of trademark infringement as 'confusion' (where the law protects the trademark owner from confusion as to the identity of the product or service that the trademark represent) to 'dilution', where the law protects the very identity of the trademark itself:

> Thus, it used to be the case that trademark infringement would only be found where the use of a protected mark by someone (X) other than its owner (Y) was likely to cause consumers to be *confused* as to the origin of the product to which the mark was attached. This issue was whether consumers would think that X's product actually came from Y. Now it is increasingly being suggested – with varying degrees of success – that if X's use of Y's signs on its product causes consumers to be reminded of Y on seeing X's product, even while knowing that X and Y are distinct trades, infringement has occurred. In other words, *creating associations between products is becoming established as the exclusive prerogative of the trademark owner*; associations created by other producers can be legally prevented if they *dilute* the first mark.
>
> (Lury, 2004: 108–9)

In absolute terms, the value of the world's 100 most valuable brands was estimated to be $434 billion in 2001, roughly 4 per cent of US GDP (at $10,400 billion in 2002), and roughly three times total US advertising expenditure (at $132 billion in 2000). While the relative weight of brands in relation to other tangible and intangible assets naturally varies in different industries, there is no doubt that brand equity represents very substantial values on today's financial markets. To some extent these brand values build on old styled salaried labour. Brands like amazon.com or heavily branded retailers like Tesco or Sainsbury's employ an army of packaging, transport and call-centre workers to produce the particular relation to consumers that the brand embodies. But the substance of brand value lies in consumer *attention*. It is what consumers think off or do with the brand that is the source of its value; it is 'what resides in the minds of customers' (Keller, 2001: 14) that makes up the most important component of what the managerial discourse calls brand equity (that is, the capacity of a brand to generate value). And this attention devoted to the brand is also what brand valuation instruments base their measurements on (see Chapter 6 for a more detailed discussion of brand valuation). To some extent, consumer attention can be produced by means of advertising, design and brand management in general. But it is generally recognized (not least by brand managers themselves, see Chapter 4) that, in the end, valuable consumer attention is the outcome of a social communication process which retains a degree of autonomy. Hence, as Chapter 4 will show, brand management is mainly about managing a productive process which is *external* to the brand-owning organization, and which cannot be controlled in its entirety. Brands are thus a good illustration of how, as Gabriel Tarde (1901, 1904) suggested long ago, more or less autonomous public communication has become a direct source of economic value. This principle – the reliance on autonomously produced externalities as a source of surplus value and profits – makes the brand a paradigmatic embodiment of the logic of informational capitalism.

Brands and informational capitalism

Brands are a form of immaterial capital; a form of 'crystallized knowledge' (or *conaissance cristallisé*), to use André Gorz's (2003: 33) term. As such they embody the fusion of the attention and the production economy, of aesthetics and economics more generally, long underway in the transition away from Fordism (Jameson, 1991; Harvey, 1991; Lash and Urry, 1994). But brands are more than that. As a sort of virtual real estate (Schiller, 1999) they occupy a valuable position in the life-world (or to use marketing terminology, the '*minds*') of consumers. That position is valuable insofar as it enables a brand to subsume and appropriate what consumers do *with the brand in mind* as source of surplus value and profits. Consequently brands work as a kind of ubiquitous managerial devices by means of which everyday life is managed, or perhaps better, programmed, so that it evolves in ways that can potentially generate the right kind of attention (and hence, brand value). As Lury (1999, 2004) argues, the brand works as a kind of platform that anticipates certain kinds of actions and attachments. Nike's efforts to make its logo condense a complex web of meanings and intensities have the effect that *with a swosh* certain actions come to assume distinct and particular meanings. The brand, Lury argues, pre-structures the action; it enters in between consciousness and the act, so to say. What brand owners *own* is a particular predetermined frame of action, a particular relation between 'action and semiosis' (ibid.: 514), between what consumers do and what their actions mean to them. Rob Shields paints a similar picture, if in more general terms. Brands, he argues, are virtual goods. With 'virtual' he means 'something that does not have the tangibility of the actual but that clearly exists none the less' (Shields, 2003: 177; see also Levy, 1998). The brand name – Nike, Rolex, Armani – anticipates future experiences and attachments. Both Lury and Shields are on to something very fundamental about the brand today: brands do not so much stand for products, as much as they provide a part of the context in which products are used. This is the core component of the use-value that brands provide consumers with. With a particular brand I can act, feel and be in a particular way. With a Macintosh computer I can become a particular kind of person, and form particular kinds of relations to others. A brand is thus nothing less than the propertied 'frame of action', to use Erving Goffman's (1974) term. This context becomes valuable in economic terms, it acquires brand equity, when it is able to reliably produce certain forms of attention, through the subsumption or (which is the same thing) management of essentially autonomous communicative processes. But contrary to our standard image of management (or the capitalist subsumption of labour as such) this process does not primarily work by means of discipline. Rather, brands work by *enabling* consumers, by empowering them in particular directions. This is different from Fordist advertising (see Chapter 3) which was primarily directed at imposing a particular structure of needs and tastes on consumers. Brands rather embrace the general principle of what Nicolas Rose (1999) has called 'advanced liberal governance' – they work *with* the freedom of con- sumers, they say not 'You Must!' but 'You May!' (Barry, 2001; Zizek, 1999).

This enabling logic is connected to the productive condition of what I will call 'informational capitalism' (Dyer-Withford, 1999; other com- mon terms are 'digital' [Schiller, 1999] or 'cognitive' [Moulier-Boutang, 2002] capitalism). Debates around the possibility of a new form of capitalism centred primarily on immaterial, informational production, rather than industrial production, have been long and complex, and are far from concluded. However, it seems that two central principles are emerging. First, the concept of 'informational capitalism' indicates a blurring of the distinction between 'production' and 'consumption' or 'circulation', that was central to theories of industrial society. This is visible in a wide variety of phenomena, such as the blurring of work and leisure that marks the lived reality of the new 'symbol analytical' professional classes, for whom the 'network sociality' of social events and the pursuit of 'culturally mobile' forms of consumption have come to feed directly into the 'entrepreneurial' production of a professional self with an attractive market position (Hage and Powers, 1992; Reich, 1991; Wittel, 1999). It is visible in aspects of the 'online economy' like dating sites or MMORPGs (Massive Multiplayer Online Role-Playing Games), where play, flirtation and other forms of user interaction is what actually produces the attractive content to which the sites in question sell access (see Chapter 6). It is visible in the growing importance of lottery games and pyramid schemes, and new forms of direct valorization of the faith and religious belief, like the prosperity gospels or the other forms of 'money magic' that have become an important aspect of 'Millennial Capitalism' (Comaroff and Comaroff, 2000). It is visible in the new strategic importance of intellectual property rights and the present tendency towards the appropriation and privatization of common resources, like genetic information or biodiversity. All of these instances illustrate how, as Comaroff and Comaroff (2000) put it, 'the workplace can no longer be privileged as the place for the production of value'. Rather, the production process now relies on and appropriates as a source of value, wealth that derives from a series of activities – playing, worshipping, wining and dining, or just looking (Beller, 2002; Lee and LiPuma, 2002) – that used to be considered part of the wasteful realm of consumption. In all of these instances, the most important source of value becomes the ability to appropriate an externality: in Morris-Suzuki's words, 'the direct exploitation of labour is becoming less important as a source of profit and the private exploitation of social knowledge is becoming more important' (1997: 64). This externality can consist in knowledge in different forms, contacts and 'social capital', fads, fashions or style and image 'capital'. For example, an art director might draw on a stylistic sensibility or a sense of *cool* that is articulated within the social networks, or the urban environment more generally, in which he or she moves. Similarly, a software engineer might appropriate innovations produced in the open source movement or draw on the free knowledge available in online discussion groups.

Although some of these externalities (such as biodiversity) can be naturally given, most are produced through one form of social

communication or another. (And, as Hardt and Negri [2004] con-
vincingly argue, the management of biodiversity or other forms of
genetic wealth relies directly on forms of productive communication.)
This then leads us on to the second emerging principle of informational
capitalism: the putting to work of communication.

This putting to work of communication has been central to what
Maurizio Lazzarato (1997) has called 'immaterial labour'. With
immaterial labour Lazzarato refers to the kinds of labour that are
employed to produce the increasingly important immaterial (aesthetic,
emotional, social) qualities of goods, or to produce and reproduce the
flexible social conditions that allow for their production. Immaterial
labour can be salaried: it can be performed by people who are formally
members of an organization. But it can also be unsalaried. It can be a
matter of the 'free labour' (Terranova, 2004; that is, free in the sense
of both unpaid and unsupervised) of net users, consumers, or online
gamers. In any case, the productivity of immaterial labour builds on the
ability of human communication to produce a surplus sociality, what
Lazzarato calls an 'ethical surplus' (drawing on Hannah Arendt who saw
the human capacity to produce a common world through communication as the foundation of the very ethical problematic). This ethical
surplus consists in a social relation, a shared meaning, or a sense of
belonging, that was not there before. In the form of a 'team spirit' a
meaning or experience attached to a brand or a subcultural style, it can
feed into the post-Fordist production process by providing a context that
makes the production or the realization of value possible. Surplus value
then becomes (partially) based on the ability of immaterial labour to
produce 'surplus community' (Lazzarato, 1997: 13). But to produce an
ethical surplus is also a feature of human communication in general. To
Hannah Arendt (1958: 183) 'action and speech produces the social'. The
core functionality of immaterial labour is thus its capacity to produce
sociality. Conceived this way it is no longer possible (as it was for Arendt)
to indicate a phenomenological difference between productive labour
and unproductive communication or consumption. This difference
becomes but a matter of function (whether a particular activity is
positioned as labour or not). Indeed, the production of economically
valuable forms of ethical surplus often proceeds through productive
practices that actively make use of consumer goods: either through
workers employing consumer goods and Media Culture 'on the job' to
form social relations (pop culture as a way of generating group solidarity), or through communicative consumer practices that unfold 'off
the job' but that produce some form of externality that can subsequently

be appropriated (teenagers using goods to produce a trend which feeds into the development of an advertising campaign). Indeed, Lazzarato argues that today, consumption should be taken as the most important manifestation of the production of an important 'surplus community' (Lazzarato, 1997: 42).

While Lazzarato talks of the productive dimension of consumption, he does not touch on one thing that has been a central concern for media studies: mediatization, and the mediatization of consumption in general. Within the theoretical framework presented by Lazzarato (and his fellow 'autonomist' Marxists; see Chapter 2) one could argue that the mediatization of social life, and of consumption in particular, has served to enhance the productivity of human communication: it has increased its potential to produce an ethical surplus.

Mediatization

Modern social theory has been premised on a distinction between, on the one hand the world of mediated communication and, on the other hand the *reality* of everyday life. *Media Culture*, the representations and symbols diffused by mass media like cinema, television, radio, advertising and the press (particularly in its low-brow, popular version – cf. Kellner, 1995) have been understood as somehow less real or authentic than the supposedly unmediated contact with 'the Real' provided by everyday praxis. The expansion of an industrialized Media Culture was thus often seen as a threat against the ability of some groups, or of people in general to 'connect with' the Real and thus articulate a realistic understanding of their actual situation. Media Culture risked alienating people from their actual conditions of existence; it worked as a kind of ideology. Today we are inclined to view this narrative as far too simplistic. We tend to argue that it rests on a romantic perception of human subjectivity that does not recognize that interaction with the Real is always somehow mediated, if nothing else by language itself. People are not angels, true understanding is impossible; ideology is a necessary element to the process of human sense-making (Althusser, 1970); distortion, selective reconstruction and the improbability of communication are part of the human condition (Luhmann, 1995; Peters, 1999). Indeed, social theorists today sometimes exaggerate in the other direction, naturalizing the extent to which our contemporary life is infused by Media Culture. Thus Paddy Scannel argues that radio and television broadcasting should be 'analysed as naturally occurring phenomena' (1996: 18) that provide us with experiences and perceptions and serve to anchor us to the Real, much like the pair of wooden clogs in van Gogh's painting, famously analysed by Heidegger (1935). Similarly, 'Neuro-aesthetics' has begun to (rather successfully) look for parallels between the generic conventions of Hollywood movies and the deep, pre-linguistic functions of the brain (Grodal, 1997).

Even if we can no longer take the naïve stance of modern critical theorists, I still think that it is possible to recognize that they *did* have a point. There is a substantial difference between the necessary mediatiz-ation of human life in general, and the historically specific mediatization that sets in with modernity. In the latter case it is a matter of an industrial-ization or technicization of mediated communication. The development of a culture industry – a process that can be said to begin with the development of mass-circulating newspapers in the nineteenth century and proceed with cinema, radio and television up to the converging mediascapes of the present day – puts in motion a process of abstraction of the symbolic languages that we employ to make sense of the world. Language becomes 'wider than human experience' to use Hanna Arendt's words (1958: 3). It is externalized from the concrete situations of everyday life. Media Culture in its present, industrialized form is an abstract discourse where the identity of the sender tends to recede into anonymity. Mediated communications tend to be perceived as a series of events, rather than as messages emanating from an identifiable sender. Moreover, these events tend to unfold in more or less complete independence from our everyday lives in a way that is very different from how orally based cultures used to work.

What marks the contemporary, post-modern condition is that the domain of objective Media Culture has expanded to infuse virtually all walks of life. It is no longer meaningful, as it might have been in the 1930s, to distinguish mediated experiences from more direct and authentic ones. We simply have very few of the latter. We continuously deploy the symbols and discourses of media culture to make do in our everyday life. When we construct our perceptions of places we visit or people we meet, when we construct friendship, declare our love or have sex, some element of Media Culture generally enters as a communicative, interpretative or inspirational device. It works as an ever-present commonly available resource – what Chapter 2 will call a 'General Intellect' (drawing on Marx) – that significantly enhances the social, sexual or romantic potential of everyday communication. This way, Scannel is of course right: broadcasting and other forms of Media Culture have become natural and necessary components of everyday life – watching television or playing computer games together is a natural way of spending quality time with one's children.

This complete integration of Media Culture and everyday life means that it no longer makes much sense to maintain a distinction between the two. Rather Media Culture is better perceived as providing an ambience (or a series of ambiences) within which life naturally occurs. The media are not so much means of communication as they are a framework, or a 'place' where we can have experiences (Bocca-Artieri, 2004; McCarthy, 2001). Everyday life unfolds within a well-nigh completely artificial environment, to a large extent constructed by objective Media Culture. In this sense, Reality Television should be considered realistic, Mark Andrejevic (2003) argues. *Big Brother* realistically depicts everyday life in its real artificiality.

This 'prodigious expansion of culture throughout the social realm' (Jameson, 1991: 4) is a result of the development of capitalism. Media Culture is commercial culture: its contents are commodified, its communications proceed in order to make money. This means that life within the media is also life within capital. The mediatization of the life-world is nothing but a consequence of the process that Marx theorized as the 'real subsumption' of life under capital; the process in which capital enters the social fabric 'vertically' to penetrate its every fibre, to become part of the very basic, bio-political conditions of life itself. In this sense, the brand as a propertied frame of action is but one aspect of a general movement towards the commodification and capitalist appropriation of the bio-political framework in which life unfolds.

The argument

The argument in this book is that brands are a paradigmatic embodiment of the logic of informational capitalism. First, because brands are in themselves immaterial, informational objects. They are part of the propertied ambience of media culture in which life unfolds. As such, brands become valuable through their ability to manage and program human communication and appropriate the ethical surplus – the common – that it produces as a source of value. This valuable common is in turn produced by people who employ the generally available General Intellect of media culture as a resource to enhance the productive potential of their communicative interaction. Brands are thus an example of capital socialized to the extent of transpiring the minute relations of everyday life, to the point of becoming a context for life, in effect. And conversely, as a capital-context, as contextual capital, brands both work as means of production to be employed in an autonomous process of constructing a common, and as embodiments of a new form of capitalist domination that governs that productive autonomy through particular kinds of empowerments. The brand, like informational capital in general, works through the bio-political context of existence to subsume the most basic and fundamental qualities of human life – the very 'naked life' of humanity, to use Agamben's (1998) term – its ability to produce a common.

This rise of the brand as a social, economic and existential reality has not been without its critics. Lately social movements have focused on brands in their critique of contemporary capitalism. This critique of brands is perhaps best expressed in Naomi Klein's recent bestseller *No Logo* (2000). Well informed and articulate, Klein uses brands as a vehicle for her denunciation of a wide range of aspects of contemporary capitalism: the colonization of the life-world by corporate power; the commercialization of arts and education; the cynical use of diversity as a marketing vehicle; the re-emergence of nineteenth-century style working conditions in the sweat-shops to which material production is out-sourced; and the concomitant disappearance of the solid blue collar jobs that once made an autonomous working class culture possible in the West. Similarly, movements like 'Ad-busters' or 'Culture Jammers' use irony or cut-up techniques to attack advertising and brand messages as the public manifestations of an invasive and unequal economic system (often to find their subversive strategies recycled as savvy advertising campaigns).

Klein continues a long tradition of critical thinkers who have denounced the irrationality of consumer capitalism. But, as she herself has said, her book is more about capitalism in general than about brands. And she does not analyse the political–economic function of the brand in depth: its status within what might very well be perceived as an emerging social and institutional order. That, on the other hand, is the task of this book: to provide a theory of the brand as a capitalist institution, and not just as a cultural phenomenon. To do that, this book starts by suggesting how the circulation of commodities can be understood as generating a series of productive practices. Chapter 2 aims at providing a theoretical framework for thinking about consumer agency within a renewed Marxist framework. The chapter argues that, although a certain creativity or agency in the use of goods or other objects has probably always been part of the human condition, this agency can be understood to have been enhanced by the process of mediatization of consumption, and in particular through the impact of electronic media. Drawing on Marx's term 'General Intellect', the chapter goes on to argue that Media Culture works as a commonly available productive force that serves to strengthen the productive powers of social interaction: its capacity to produce a *common*.

Chapters 3 through 5 look at the other side of the matter: how capital has developed strategies to valorize the diffuse productivity of consumption. Traditionally, Marxists have concentrated on management as the chief capitalist discipline of valorization. Chapter 3 departs from that tradition by instead concentrating on marketing, and tracing the origins of the contemporary brand management paradigm. It argues that the development of twentieth-century marketing largely follows that of management. Up until the 1950s, marketing was largely conceived as a matter of imposing particular needs and desires on consumers, much like Taylorist management worked to impose particular work-practices through discipline. But, beginning in the late 1950s, marketing began to abandon its disciplinary focus to open up to the actual complexity of consumer practices. It now became important to observe, learn from and incorporate the actual meanings and practices that people articulated around goods. Marketing began to recognize that the emerging autonomous productivity of consumers could be configured as an important economic resource. The chapter shows how the crucial factor behind this development was the transformation of the informational interface of marketing. This in turn was an outcome of marketing's reaction to the changes in consumer practice induced by electronic media. Chapters 4 and 5 examine contemporary practices of brand management. Chapter 4 begins by looking at the branding of consumer goods. It argues that contemporary brand management contains two sets of techniques. One set aims at the commodification of the autonomous productivity of consumers as it unfolds naturally in its social environment. Examples are techniques like cool hunting and viral marketing that address particularly productive and 'culturally mobile' consumers. Another set of techniques aims at anticipating and programming the productivity of consumers and guiding it in particular directions. This constitutes the core of contemporary brand management and involves advertising and other forms of media positioning, the construction of brand communities and other forms of Customer Relationship Management and the use of branded spaces. These techniques address the mass of ordinary consumers whose productivity, autonomy and cultural mobility are more limited. They aim at anticipating and shaping their use of branded goods so that it serves to reproduce a particular brand identity. Chapter 4 concludes with a look at corporate and political branding. It argues that today management has taken on techniques of branding, to constitute the corporation as a particular form of brandspace where the autonomous productivity of co-workers is made to unfold in a particular direction, towards the creation of particular, valuable forms of meaning and social relations. The chapter suggests that in these practices, as in political branding proper, it is a matter of putting the political potential of human communication to work. Chapter 5 examines branding strategies on the internet. It argues that new Information and Communication Media work as a kind of technological extension of the logic of brand management. These media make it particularly feasible to construct ambiences in which communication is pre-structured to unfold in particular dimensions. This principle of providing ambiences for the exercise of 'controlled forms of freedom' is emerging as a key principle of the internet economy. The second part of the chapter examines plans for a future mobile internet. It shows how the extensions of these ambiences and their fusion with everyday life points at an emerging contradiction in which the capitalist logic of control and automation threatens to marginalize the very consumer productivity on which the commercial logic behind these technologies rests. Chapter 6, the conclusion, expands on the ways in which brands offer an understanding of the central logic and emerging contradictions of informational capitalism.

2 Consumption

During the last thirty years or so, consumption has been established on the agenda of the social sciences. To many contemporary thinkers, consumption, and related questions of culture and identity appear to be the best point of entry in understanding present social relations, while production has been superseded. (Indeed, Daniel Miller [1997] proposes that an adequate understanding of contemporary capitalism might do well with departing from consumption, rather than production.) The rise of consumption on the agenda of social theory has correlated with the discovery of the 'active consumer'. It was only when the Cultural Studies tradition of the 1970s had established that consumers are not 'passive dopes' of mass culture, but that they act, resist and exercise creativity in their consumer practices, that consumption became an interesting area of study in its own right. Before the mid-1970s (and with the exception of American sociologists like Gans [1966], Rainwater et al. [1959] and Warner [1949]), the assumption had been that consumption was a passive and private pursuit, largely unrelated to the social world that constituted the object domain of the social sciences. Like most Marxists, social scientists in general thought of consumption as the end station of production in which 'the product steps out of the social movement and becomes a direct object and servant of individual need, and satisfies it in being consumed' (Marx, 1973[1939]: 89).[2] As a 'terminal point' and 'end in itself' consumption belongs outside of the realm of economics (and social science) and whatever drives it ('needs arising from the stomach or from the imagination', Marx, 1990[1867]: 125) has no bearing on the analysis of political economy. As an interest in consumption as a creative practice spread from cultural studies proper to sociology, anthropology, history and, ultimately, 'Critical Consumer Studies' – an offshoot of the academic discipline of marketing (that discipline had previously been dominated by cognitive psychology and information processing theory;

cf. Cochoy, 1999; Miller, 1995) – a corresponding emphasis on the 'agency' or even 'resistance' of consumers was maintained, sometimes to the point of producing a discourse that had uncanny similarities with contemporary Thatcherite enthusiasm about the sovereign consumer (cf. McGuigan, 1992; Morris, 1992). Often, the emphasis on consumer agency was used as an anti-Marxist point. This became particularly prominent in the 1980s, as the original neo-Gramscian perspective of the Birmingham school of Cultural Studies was supplanted by feminist and post-structuralist influences. Mica Nava, for example, argues that the 'totalizing perspective' of 'Marxists of the Frankfurt School' has worked as an obstacle to the search for adequate understandings of contemporary consumer practice, as it has given too little space for such necessary agency. In Marxist analyses of advertising, she argues, this has been constructed as a 'monolithic force, which the helpless consumer/spectator/subject is incapable of resisting' (Nava, 1997: 36). It is true that 'Marxists of the Frankfurt School' (I gather that Nava thinks of Adorno, who was not, strictly speaking, a Marxist) or of other denominations (like Baran and Sweezy [1966] or Mandel [1975], who arguably were the first Marxists to give consumption a place in the analysis of contemporary capitalism) have given little attention to the actual complexities of consumer behaviour. In general they tended to treat consumption as wasteful or irrational, devoted to the pursuit of the useless ('kitsch in the living room'), the dangerous ('cigarettes') or the frivolous and artificial (fashion or new car models; cf. Mandel, 1975: 399). But, I suggest that Marx should not be discarded entirely. A different, more contemporary reading of Marx can give us a better, more sociological understanding of the concept that contemporary studies of consumption puts at the centre of its analysis, yet practically never defines: Consumer Agency.

Consumer agency

Virtually all students of contemporary consumer practice agree that consumers use goods productively; they use them to construct social relations, shared emotions, personal identity or forms of community (they 'make love in supermarkets' to use Daniel Miller's [1998] fortunate phrase). Within academic consumer research it has become 'normal science' to argue that consumption is a productive practice. Consumption is a 'critical site in which identities, boundaries and shared meanings are forged' (Kates, 2002). Bernard and Veronique Cova argue that for many consumers, the main use-value of consumer goods is their 'linking values', or their capacity to mediate and cement the social relations that make up the context of consumption (Cova and Cova, 2001; Cova, 1997). This seems to be the case not only in particular subcultures, like gays (Kates, 1998), fundamentalist Christians (O'Guinn and Belk, 1989), 'natural health' enthusiasts (Thompson and Troester, 2002), skydivers (Celsi *et al.*, 1993), Harley Davidson enthusiasts (Shouten and McAlexander, 1995) and *Star Trek* enthusiasts (Kozinets, 2001). Also for more 'ordinary' or 'straight' people, consumption is a central locus for the production of community. As Muniz and O'Guinn (2001) note, ordinary suburban Americans readily form communities around brands like Saab, Bronco or Macintosh. These communities are significant social formations, maintained through investments in face-to-face and online interaction, and they generate moral ties and a sense of mutual commitment:

> Consider Jill's comments on what she considers (more than half seriously) to be a moral failing of a former employee who switched to an IBM clone. 'Skip used to be a Mac person, but switched. I found this morally reprehensible. . . . He's kind of a Mac turncoat.' Skip had joined the ranks of PC users, and Jill believes that this affected their personal relationship. Jill also sees Skip as a defector from a like-minded social group (community). In a similar fashion, Saab community members resent Saab drivers moving to another car and apply corrective coercion to prevent them from doing so. One informant, Mary, refers to one Saab driver who left the fold as having betrayed the brotherhood.
>
> (Muinz and O'Guinn, 2001: 428)

Muniz and O'Guinn go on to claim that 'attempts to build community through consumption practices are more than mere compensatory acts' (2001: 415). They are creative and productive practices from which genuinely new forms of community emerge. As Russell Belk argued already in 1988, consumption should be understood as a practice in which consumers construct themselves and the common social world that connects them to each other (Belk, 1988). In short, consumption should be understood as a site for the production of what Michael Hardt and Antonio Negri (2004) have quite simply called a *common*.[3] Consequently the use-values of consumer goods should be conceived as something more than their ability to respond to extra-social needs or desires (coming from the 'stomach or the fancy'). Rather, recent consumer research would prove that these use-values consist mainly in the qualities of goods as means of production: their capacity to be deployed within an ongoing immaterial production process by means of which such a common is constructed. The use-value of goods comes not primarily from their ability to cater to passive pleasures – the autonomous imaginative hedonist daydreaming, that Colin Campbell (1987) famously put at the heart of modern consumerism – but from their ability to be deployed within productive consumer practice (Firat and Schutz, 1997; Holt, 1997).

Where then does this active, productive consumer, this *bricoleur* (de Certeau, 1984), come from? That question remains unclear. To most contemporary consumer scholars, the active use of consumer goods (or of objects or media texts in general) is something close to a universal human trait. To the post-structuralists it has to do with the universal human tendency to differ (or to *differance*, to use a term made popular by Derrida; Denzin, 2001). Historians have contributed to reinforce the idea of the universality of consumer agency, by showing how early modern consumers were no 'cultural dopes' but made active use of goods in the construction of social relations and forms of identity (cf. Brewer and Porter, 1993; Finn, 2004; Roche, 2000; Sassatelli, 2004). Indeed, one can find many examples of 'consumer agency' before its discovery by Cultural Studies in the 1970s. Although it has been common to associate innovative consumer practices with the upper classes (while the middle to lower classes have been thought to simply imitate these innovations; cf. Simmel, 1904;, Veblen, 1899), recent historiography has stressed how at a relatively early stage, such practices had begun to acquire a mass appeal (De Vries, 1993). Proletarian consumers seemed particularly eager to make unexpected and sometimes spectacular use of consumer goods (Berg and Clifford, 1999: 8). During the second half of the nineteenth century, young American working class women 'began to militantly assert their own brand of class and gender pride by boldly rejecting middle-class styles of femininity in favour of gaudy colours, outrageous accessories and (relatively) low skirts and dresses which accentuated their hips and thighs'. At the same time, young working class male dandies, 'B'hoys', walked the streets of New York with 'lavishly greased, long front locks, black, broad-rimmed hats, turned down shirt collars, black frock-coats with skirts below the knee, embroidered shirts, tight pantaloons, ever present cigars' and a 'profusion of jewellery as varied and costly as the b'hoy could procure' (Swiencicki, 1999: 221, ff.; cf. Stansell, 1986). The middle classes, on the other hand, practised restraint in their consumer patterns – Kuchta (1996, drawing on Vügel's early work on 'the psychology of clothing') has labelled the modesty that marked English nineteenth-century men's fashions as 'the great sartorial renunciation'. For both the middle class and the working class, consumer culture became an important arena for the forging of class identity.

On the other hand, it is striking how the contemporary discovery of 'the active consumer' was associated with very particular sociological conditions. True, to some extent this 'discovery' had political reasons. The Cultural Studies tradition emerged with the discovery of the political relevance of everyday life on the part of scholars like Richard Hoggart (1957), Raymond Williams (1958) and E.P. Thompson (1968). They wrote in a time when working class communities seemed seriously threatened by an invasive commercial culture. Their political aims were principally to finds ways to resist this movement (although not necessarily by conserving 'working class culture' as it might once have been). During the 1970s and 1980s, however, it became increasingly obvious that such non-consumerist cultures no longer existed. There was simply nothing outside of the 'candy-floss world' – to use Hoggart's expression – of consumer capitalism that could resist. Or, to put it in Paul Willis' words, 'commercial cultural commodities are all that most people have' (1990: 26). Resistance, quite simply had to be found within consumer culture, first with youth, then with women and lately, with people *qua* consumers. But, at the same time, two conditions were common to all the subjects investigated by the Cultural Studies scholars of the 1970s (and, I would argue to ordinary consumers today): first, their lack of a clearly defined identity, or 'role' to appropriate and make their own. While Talcott Parsons (1942[1964]) could argue in the 1940s that the consumer practices of American youth served to prepare them for adult (WASP, middle class) life, as youth culture replicated the values of adult society, this was no longer true in the 1970s. Rather, it is striking how the youth cultures analysed by Hall and Jefferson in their *Resistance through Rituals* (1975) were all about constructing either an alternative to a working class culture that was crumbling under the pressures of industrial restructuring (this was perhaps most prevalent in the case of the Skinheads, whose attempts to reconstruct a vanishing working class masculinity had developed into a kind of fetishism), or, as in the case of the 'Mods', a new middle class culture of consumerism for which there was virtually no precedent (cf. Polhemus, 1994). The construction of subcultures, they argued, 'provided an answer to the problem of alienation' (Clarke *et al.*, 1975: 29). It was the homelessness or lack of an obvious place that made consumers make productive use of goods. (And as Chapter 4 will argue, it is the labour power of the most alienated consumers that remains most valuable to brand managers today.) This was true also for the feminist analysis that followed. To Angela McRobbie, young girls used *Jackie* magazine to construct an identity that could offer an alternative to the 'the class based and oppressive features of the school' from which they were profoundly alienated (McRobbie,

1990). To Janice Radway, it was the lack of a place of one's own, to which one could retreat from the suffocating demands of one's family, that made 'romance readers . . . use their books to erect a barrier between themselves and their families in order to declare themselves temporarily off-limits to those who would mine them for emotional support and material care' (Radway, 1984[1991]: 12). For the sub-cultures of the 1970s (as for the proletarian consumers of the nineteenth century) consumer agency emerged as a response to the lack of clear identity and social position, the becoming contingent on the context of action and sense-making.

The second common factor was the sheer availability of tools to use in such productive consumer practices. Dick Hebdidge (1979) underlined this in his analysis of the Punk movement. The symbolic *bricolage* that stood at the heart of the 'practice of punk' was ultimately made possible by the mountain of debris – military boots, S&M collars, bikers' jackets, safety pins – that could be appropriated and recycled, and not least by the new ubiquity of electronic media, record players, electronic instruments and recording devices, portable PAs, and so on. Indeed, one could argue that the very emergence of a generational youth identity in the mid-1950s was contingent on a new availability of consumer goods and new media technologies. The core of the youth culture, the global music market, was made possible by television, where programme like *American Bandstand* rapidly diffused novelties to a mass market, and the durable 45 rpm record that permitted a much closer integration of music into everyday life. The result was that music came to enter a series of new social practices – dating, driving, partying – and consequently, that the speed of innovation in music styles (mixed genres, new dances, and so on) accelerated (Burnett, 1996: 1; Chaffee, 1985; Longhurst, 1995; Sanjek, 1996).

The integration and successive transnational circulation of new consumer practices – white teenagers experimenting with black music, the British pop scene (themselves enabled by new electronic instruments and recording technologies) – made the music industry into the dynamic hub of the 'global ecumene' (Hannerz, 1992) of youth culture, involving other media texts like films and magazines, as well as fashions and consumer goods marketed directly at youth (clothes, sports equipment, soft drinks). In various combinations, these objects and texts were appropriated in the production of new forms of identity and sociality: rock and roll, motorbikes and leather for the bikers; Motown soul, Italian fashion and scooters for the Mods; Grateful Dead, ethnic fashions and hallucinogenic drugs for the hippies, and so on. In all of these instances, consumer goods were employed as a resource in the production of identities and forms of sociality that somehow resisted or evaded the code of value of 'mass society'. This role of consumer goods as an important means of production was also evident in the politicization of youth culture that occurred in the second half of the 1960s. Certain garments, like jeans, army parkas and certain genres of commercial music, like American 'folk' music, became indispensable elements to the very performance of opposition. Indeed, in many ways it was the universal nature of these objects and texts – a universality acquired through mediatization – that provided a global coherence to the great variety of actions that made up 'The Sixties' (Eyerman and Jamison, 1994; Lumley, 1990; Marwick, 1998). What the nation, the party and the union had done for the politicized working class of the early years of the century, consumer goods did for their grandchildren: it gave a sense of coherence, of being part of a movement, a set of common rituals, the means to perform a common identity. So it seems that the increased mediatization of consumer goods and of social life in general could also have played a part in rendering consumer practices productive.

At the same time, these innovations were rapidly appropriated and transformed into new market niches. The music industry actively surveyed youthful innovations and incorporated the results as new market niches. When the system stabilized in the 1960s, Middleton (1990: 15) argues, the productivity of youth culture was positioned as an internal element to the productive circle of the music industry, and, consequently, a productive or at least 'interactive attitude was inscribed in the context of music consumption as such. Something similar happened to mainstream, middle class consumer culture during the 1960s, and it was linked to the impact of electronic media.

Electronic media

Marshall McLuhan had famously heralded the transforming impact of electronic media (by which he chiefly meant television). New media would quickly render American culture more participatory and intimate, and help overcome the distance created (in bourgeois Man) by print technology and the 'acting without reacting' that it fostered (McLuhan, 1964: 4). This shift would be particularly prevalent in consumer practice, McLuhan argued, where a utilitarian, iconic age would be replaced by a sensual and tactile one, able to appreciate the new 'sculptural spaces in cars, clothes and housing' (ibid.: 131). While McLuhan's predictions were clearly exaggerated, and while they tended to conflate social, economic and cultural change into the simple shift over from radio to television, they did contain a grain of truth. American consumer culture did become more participatory and activated under the impact of television and the new Media Culture that formed around that technology. Once again, the obvious objection would be that this was nothing new and there had been many well documented instances of productive consumer agency in the past, like in the case of young women or 'flappers' who in the inter-war years enacted a new female identity centred on new consumer goods like lipstick or silk stockings, new practices (dancing, cocktails, smoking) and new media (cinema, weekly magazines; Peiss, 1986; de Grazia, 1992), of movie fandom (Barday, 2001) and of first and second generation immigrants appropriating mainstream American goods to enact their own identities (Cohen, 1990). But, from the point of view of the marketing profession at least, these had all been conceived as marginal phenomena or as disturbances to be corrected. It was assumed that most ordinary (white, middle class) consumers derived their sense of taste and utility from socially anchored consumption norms that had been constructed independently of the influence of goods and Media Culture. If anything, the task of marketing was that of overcoming such pre-consumerist, irrational preference structures, and imposing a common consumption norm on the recalcitrant masses (see next chapter). This way marketing did not particularly encourage consumer agency. But with the new suburban middle class that began to make its presence felt in the second half of the 1950s, marketing met with an important, indeed trend-setting social group, for whom the construction of new forms of social relations and identity through the productive use of consumer goods had become standard practice.

This was particularly prevalent from the many studies on 'The New Suburbia' undertaken by sociologists and market researchers in the American 1950s. In official pictures, American 1950s middle class consumer culture seemed to leave little room for individuality or difference. The new American suburban consumers, who although they were not a majority came to stand for the 'New Consumer' as such, appeared to be an epitome of conformity, ruled by the necessity to 'keep up with the Joneses' (a device made famous by economist Duesenberry's 1949 theory of the 'demonstration effect') and the concomitant need to keep up appearances and subdue individuality (Coontz, 1992). Sociologist William H. Whyte, who when not proclaiming the dismal era of the *Organization Man* (Whyte, 1956) participated in the *Fortune* magazine study of the 'Consumer in the New Suburbia' ('A preview of what lies ahead'), identified what he called 'keeping down with the Joneses'; avoiding conspicuous consumption in order not to break with the 'communal ethic' as the most powerful sociological force in the life of the suburban consumer (Whyte, 1955). However, other market reports stressed that beneath this strong communal discipline there were small differences that marketers should be sensitive to. Indeed, suburban consumers possessed a high sensitivity for small distinctions in style and taste that were used to articulate individuality and diversity (Paranara, 1958). The 'Interurbia report', a joint effort between Yale University, *Fortune* magazine and the J. Walter Thompson (JWT) advertising agency, discovered that 'beneath the surface of uniformity' there were 'different communities catering to different lifestyles'. Suburban women possessed strong social skills that they used in deploying consumer goods to mark off their own families from the crowd (JWT, 1957). Consumer goods, their use and display, were essential to the production of neighbourly relations in the new suburbia. This appeared to be true for the construction of identity and sense of self as well, at least for women. (Male consumer practice remained under-studied.) Cooking, or so market researchers argued, was no longer so much a matter of fulfilment of family needs as it was a question of self-expression.

As in the case of the youth cultures of the 1970s this had in part to do with the lack of a given identity. The upwardly mobile middle classes had taken the trip from the city centre to suburbia, and often from a working class home (via university and the G.I. Bill) to a managerial job. But it was also contingent on a new availability of goods. With more varied diets and the availability of exotic ingredients its 'traditional nature was breaking down' and as the British Bureau of Market Research (1961) argued, there were 'signs of an increasingly creative attitude to cooking'. Edgar Morin made similar observations in his study of the small Breton village of Plodémet: diets were becoming more varied, Italian ravioli and packaged paella began to appear at groceries. People began to drink beer, soda, aperitifs and whisky (Morin, 1967: 149). Increasingly, foods were marketed as tools for self-expression rather than just means for the satisfaction of family needs, and women's magazines began to feature more exotic and varied recipes, and celebrate the expressive joys of cooking.

Advertising, design and marketing soon embraced and encouraged this new productive use of goods. Cosmetics advertising anticipated new forms of female performative consumption by addressing a woman consumer seeking to express her own individuality and diversity (Arvidsson, 2000; McFeely, 2000; Wildt, 1998). New materials like plastics bended to any fashion and came in any shape, from imitation wood to juice containers in the size of large bright oranges (Meikle, 1995). 'Styling' put tail fins on automobiles and chrome accessories on aerodynamic domestic appliances. Dior style 'New Look' fashions, and Italian *prêt a porter* gave both a plasticity and a new visibility to women's bodies (White, 2000). Domestic appliances like see-through ovens and television-shaped washing machines and refrigerators, and the new importance of visual presentation in Betty Crocker-style cooking made 'looking and viewing central acts of consciousness' in the home (Marling, 1994: 14, ff.). The refrigerator worked as a kind of display case, showing off affluence in the form of elaborately packaged goods (Bowlby, 2000: 150). In short 'popolux': 'glitter and glimmer for the masses', radically increased the visual presence of objects in American middle class life, as represented in Hollywood cinema from *The Giant* to *Forbidden Planet* (Hine, 1986; Worland and Slayden, 2000). In a similar way, the shopping mall enriched the shopping experience, making it a space for fantasy and imagination, as well as a significant aspect of the social life of the suburban couple (JWT, 1957).

However, the most radical transformation of consumer culture came with the emergence of a new, and more differentiated media environment, structured around television. With television media culture became less spectacular, and more mundane. Television provided a sort of ambience for life; as Marshall McLuhan stressed, television would tend to present new goods as natural parts of social processes, rather than as attributes of distant personalities, like the movie stars. Although magazines still attracted a larger share of advertising revenue, television advanced rapidly to become the most important medium of mass advertising, reaching 90 per cent of all American households by 1961 (Sterling and Kitross, 1990). Expanding television ownership also changed the place of the set in everyday life. By 1962, market researchers Ira Glick and Sydney Levy argued, the feeling of novelty and excitement had worn off and television had become an integrated element of everyday life. Television sets were moved from 'the home's public and prominently displayed locations to its more private, casual, utilitarian and convenient parts' (Glick and Levy, 1962: 32). They argued that television now began to function as a source of information rather than as a form of escapism. On television the suburban middle class learned about new products, how they could be used, what they could signify. In his recent history of American television advertising, Samuel argues that 'television advertising was part of the larger standardization of American consumer culture in the post-war era, when national brands, retailers, franchises and chains flattened out regional differences and ridged demographic diversity' (2001: x). To some extent this observation is certainly valid: corporate sponsorship produced a close integration of programming and promotion that presented consumer goods as natural components of the world of 'homogenous landscapes and smiling self-satisfied WASP families' that early 1960s television presented (Jones, 1992: 33, 87; Desjardins, 1999). However (as Samuel himself observes), the mediatization of consumer culture through television also significantly altered the signifying potential of goods.

> Trained in the conventions of radio, show hosts such as Jack Benny, Arthur Godfrey and Jack Paar delivered the sponsor's commercials from the stage, effortlessly weaving between showmanship and salesmanship. Guest stars ranging from Frank Sinatra to Jerry Lewis also integrated product plugs into their performances, sewing a seamless quilt of creativity and advertising. . . . This mixing and matching of entertainment and advertising brought together the realms of popular culture . . . and consumer culture . . . in new and powerful ways.
>
> (Samuel, 2001: xvi)

Television efficiently inserted goods to the signifying networks of media culture, and weaved those networks into the environment of everyday life.

During the 1960s, there was also an accelerating differentiation of the media environment. Magazines had begun this process, catering to niche markets in response to the rise of television as a medium of mass advertising. In the early 1960s American network television abandoned the sponsorship model in favour of a 'scatter plan', where advertising time was sold in 60, 30 or even 10 second spots that spread among different programmes. This led to a greater interest in audience differentiation as advertisers were now able to reach different consumer groups by placing ads in different programmes (Men on *ABC Monday Night Football* and Housewives on daytime television). Towards the second half of the 1960s, this tended to increase the diversity of television. Programming like *Peyton Place* and *Cosmopolitan* contributed to launching the new 'Single Girl' life-style. *I Spy* (NBC, 1963–68), *Julia* (CBS, 1968) and *Mod Squad* (ABC, 1968) featured black and white actors together and tried self-consciously to further the concerns of the civil rights movement. *The New People* (ABC, 1968) represented the demeanour and aesthetics of the youthful counter-culture (Jones, 1992: 189). Together these programmes diversified the cultural universe of television and gave place for advertising targeting particular market segments. Advertisers adapted by developing the 'life-style format', where products were linked to a particular and often imaginary form of life that consumers were invited to perform. Print media also reorganized and new life-style magazines promoted themselves as vehicles of playful, expressive consumerism. The publishers had begun to target niche markets already in the early 1960s, mainly as a response to the rise of television as a medium for mass advertising. In the second half of the decade, however, publications like *Playboy, Cosmopolitan* and *Ebony* became virtual instruction manuals for living, promoting their own style as a network of practices, objects and media texts: *Playboy*, for example promoted a middle class bachelor hedonism made up by promiscuous sex, James Bond, gourmet cooking, hi-fi equipment, sport cars, Norman Mailer, liberal politics and jazz (Osgerby, 2001). In the 1970s, a mass market for men's fashions would alter the performance of middle class masculinity (Nixon, 1996). Transformations in retailing, the emergence of boutiques and the diversification of food styles brought about by supermarkets would further direct middle class consumerism away from the reproduction of traditionally sanctioned tastes and towards the productive performance of diversity.

During the 1950s through the 1970s the new electronic media landscape, together with the rise of the new middle class led to a reorientation of mainstream consumer practice. The kinds of active, participatory consumer practices that previously had been the business of the elites or the *avant garde*, now became part of the expected mainstream attitude. New products, new marketing strategies, and the new environment made agency a programmed feature of mainstream consumer culture.

This anticipation of consumer agency on a mass scale was a direct outcome of the new forms of mediatization of consumption made possible by electronic media. Pre-war, print based advertising had positioned goods as part of a spectacular culture of modernity that invited imitation or wholesale embracement. But the electronic media environment that developed in the post-war years worked differently. In part it was a matter of new media technologies entering deeper into everyday life and inviting themselves to be deployed productively in new social circumstances, as in the case of record players, Polaroid cameras and later tape and video recorders and home studio equipment. All of these functioned as tools that could be deployed productively in a wide variety of social situations. This tendency would be even clearer with the networked information technologies that emerged in the 1990s. In part it was a matter of new production and consumption technologies that permitted a greater range of diversity and, consequently, new kinds of experimentation, as in the case of the introduction of deep-freeze technology, which in combination with electronic ovens (and latter microwave ovens) significantly expanded the range of options that met the individual shopper. (Frozen microwavable meals were the main channel for introducing 'ethnic' cuisine – like Italian, Mexican and Indian dishes – into British households in the 1990s; Oddy, 2003: 192). But more than anything else, the new, more diversified media environment made a wider range of information and knowledge available and actively catered to an experimenting, interactive attitude. Cooking programmes (made more attractive by colour television) introduced a wider variety of cooking styles and recipes and encouraged imitation and experimentation. Food and wine journalism grew out of cooking programmes and fostered an attitude of active information seeking and deployment on the part of middle class consumers. Beginning in the 1980s, food and wine journalists, celebrity chefs and television personalities together with the supermarkets, did an impressive job in educating the British middle classes into wine consumers that were capable of distinguishing between and experiencing wine in a much more sophisticated manner than before. Similar things happened to fashion clothing, home technology, music, and most recently antiques. The mediatization of consumption created a commonly available informational environment that made resources that primarily had been private, the outcome of good breeding, or what Pierre Bourdieu (1984) called 'class habitus', public: generally available in the public domain. To be able to distinguish between wines it was no longer necessary to have been born into the *haute bourgeoisie*, it was enough to subscribe to *Wine Spectator*. This making private competences public and generally accessible greatly enhanced the scope and productivity of consumer agency. Concomitantly, 'cultural mobility' – the ability to move between and show mastery of a wide range of different consumer domains, and to successfully manipulate goods and symbols – began to replace proficiency in one dominant aesthetic as the main strategy of distinction (Emmison, 2003). A good middle class consumer was no longer simply someone who knew how to act (or cook, or dress) the right way, but someone who was able to put the generally available resources of a highly mediatized consumer culture to use in producing something creative, original, or at least personal (Featherstone, 1991; Firat and Schutz, 1997; Holt, 1997).

This way, the actual production process could be extended to include investments of consumers agency: consumers were invited to complete the product themselves, either materially (as in the case of interactive ready made foods) or symbolically (as in the case of mass fashions). As Chapter 4 will describe, such programmed interactivity rose to become the core principle of contemporary brand management.

General Intellect

What then does this have to do with Marx? On a first level, the extension of Media Culture and its close integration into everyday life can be understood as the completion of what Marx called the 'real subsumption' of society under capital.[4] Capital (in the form of propertied symbols, and signifying complexes: advertising, brands, television series, music and other forms of content) is socialized to the extent of it becoming part of the very environment, the bio-political context in which life is lived. The other side to this equation is that life comes to evolve entirely within capital, that there is no longer any outside. The contemporary individual is born and bred within capital, 'his' subjectivity socialized to the point of him becoming a mere medium for the circulation of value. Docile and malleable she functions as an element of the society-wide exchange of meanings and symbols where 'everything that is used as a unity by the system, is produced as a unity by the system', to use Niklas Luhmann's device.

Now this position is fairly well known and established. Some version or another of the real subsumption thesis has been central to dystopian critiques of consumer capitalism from Horkheimer and Adorno (1944) to Baudrillard (1970). Usually, the consequences have been quite dire, alienation, the end of the subject or even the end of the real. But is it possible to think another outcome of the process of real subsumption, and its consequence: the complete integration of Media Culture into everyday life?

Such a different approach can build on a perspective that been developed by the (mainly) Italian school of 'autonomist' Marxism, which developed in the post-war years (for English overviews, see Wright, 2002; Dyer-Withford, 1999). Like Baudrillard (and many others), scholars in this tradition have emphasized how the central tendency in the transition away from Fordism has been the progressive socialization of capital, and the concomitant extension of the production process 'beyond the factory gates', to encompass series of communicative and reproductive activities that were previously thought to belong to the unproductive realm of circulation. This came forth most clearly in the 1970s studies of the new Toyotist factories (that relied on self-organizing teams) and new Italian industrial districts that, at the time, promised a new wave of economic development. It seemed that much of the success of these new institutions resulted from the flexibility and adaptability that derived from the self-organization of the productive process. In the Toyotist factory the self-organizing team could respond rapidly enough to keep production 'just in time'. In the industrial district the co-operation between firms in terms of marketing and the distribution of labour power and other resources enabled it to 'breath with the market' and stay on top of a rapidly shifting demand (Marrazzi, 1999a; Bagnasco, 1977; Piore and Sabel, 1984). Clearly, this self-organization of production required other resources than the disciplined Taylorist production process. It put to work the communicative and social skills of workers, their capacity to create a (more or less stable and enduring) common social world. Negri (1989) talked about the emergence of a new form of worker that he called the 'social' or 'socializing' worker (*operaio sociale*)[5] whose main productive asset was his or her ability to put communicative action to work in producing a mobile and dynamic context in which material production could unfold. The socializing worker thus worked with a common capacity to create meaning and social relations through communication. In this she mobilized what Marx denoted with a concept dear to the Italian autonomists, General Intellect.

With General Intellect Marx meant a productive power that develops within capital. When labour is subsumed under capital, it is subjected to its discipline. Here, as in the case of the disciplinary power described more generally by Foucault, discipline works through individualization and spatial recomposition (Foucault, 1975). This is most obvious, perhaps in the case of Taylorism, probably the most advanced expression of the 'real subsumption' of labour in industrial capitalism. There, the inherent, personal knowledge of workers is replaced by a detailed scheme elaborated by the discipline of time-motion studies. Through a set of extremely detailed regulations, workers are made to move their bodies according to that scheme, to behave (rather than act) as 'moments' of a production process that is not of their own making. Under Taylorism, labour is also silenced. As in Foucault's famous image of a public lecture in a French nineteenth-century prison (where each prisoner listens to the lecturer in his own wooden box, unable to communicate with, even see his neighbour), serious effort is made to limit worker interaction on the factory floor. But, at the same time, Marx, like Foucault, recognizes that capitalist discipline is not only repressive, but also *productive*. One form of subjectivity, based in pre-capitalist social relations is repressed and another form emerges: one form of communication, mediated by the linguistic codes of the worker's own popular culture is silenced but another form of communication, mediated by machinery and the overall organization of the factory comes forth. Through the new forms of mediation that it realizes, capitalist discipline produces a new productive power, what Marx calls 'social, socialized [i.e. collective] labour' (Marx,

1990[1867]: 1024). Social labour emerges already with the organized co-operation and division of labour in early manufacture: 'Not only do we have here an increase in the productive power of the individual by means of cooperation, but the creation of a new productive power, which is intrinsically a collective one' (Marx, 1990[1867]: 443). It becomes central with 'the specifically capitalist mode of production'; industrial production deploying advanced machinery and working on a scale large enough to systematically employ scientific knowledge.

Marx develops this line of thinking to its logical conclusion in a passage often used by the Italian autonomists and retrospectively titled 'The Fragment on Machinery' (Marx, 1973[1939]: 699–706). There, Marx introduces a concept of General Intellect. With this term Marx seems, at a first glance to refer to the enormous productive powers that now appear as a property of large scale industrial capital, principally embodied in machinery. Indeed, with the development of large scale industry, the productive powers of the machinery itself effectively dwarf those of the human capacities of the worker: 'to the degree that large industry develops, the creation of real wealth comes to depend less on labour time and on the amount of labour employed than on the power of the agencies set in motion during labour time'. But, he adds, machines are no natural products, they are rather 'organs of the human brain', 'the power of knowledge, objectified' (Marx, 1973[1939]: 706). But, it is not so much a matter of the individual knowledge of the craft worker, a knowledge that was his personal property, as much as it is a matter of 'general social knowledge'. Indeed the foundation of wealth is no longer so much the direct theft of labour time, as much as the 'appropriation of [the worker's] general productive power, his understanding of nature and his mastery over it by virtue of his presence as a social body' (Marx, 1973[1939]: 705). It is his participation in the social productive power – the General Intellect – realized within capital ('created by large scale industry itself'; ibid.: 705), 'in a word, the development of the social individual which appears as the great foundation-stone of production and of wealth' (ibid.). Machinery is but one of the embodiments of a set of general competences – a general intellect – which arises from and is inscribed in the social reality of the factory system. Where then do these competences come from? One answer would be to point to the individual geniuses of science or great inventors of managerial discipline (like Taylor). But Marx's answer is different; he argues that the General Intellect should be regarded as a reality that emerges from the social organization of the productive system itself. The competences that it embodies arise from social interaction and communication within the productive process. At the same time as the 'surplus labour of the mass has ceased to be the condition for the development of general wealth' so also 'non-labour of the few' has ceased to be the foundation for the 'development of the general powers of the human head' (Marx, 1973[1939]: 705). The General Intellect, the most important force of production of late capitalism is then an emergent effect of social inter-action, beyond the direct control or command of any single individual. It evolves from the basic human capacity (and need) to form social inter-course, as this capacity is *mediated* by machinery, advanced production systems, and the socialization of capital in general.

The General Intellect thus refers to a productive resource that is generally available insofar as it is inscribed within the very environment of the productive process. Indeed, 'the development of fixed capital indicates to what degree general social knowledge has become a direct force of production' (ibid.: 706). It follows that the completion of the process of the real subsumption of social life, insofar as this means a socialization of capital to the point that it becomes a context for life, entails extension of the General Intellect to encompass not only the productive environment of the factory system, but the general environ-ment of life itself. This is precisely the point of the Italian autonomists. Like Paolo Virno, they argue that:

> Marx completely identified the general intellect (or, knowledge as the principal productive force) with fixed capital, thus neglecting the instance when that same general intellect manifests itself on the contrary as *living labour*. This is precisely the decisive aspect today. The nexus between knowledge and production is not exhausted in the system of machines; rather it is necessarily articulated through concrete subjects. Today it is not difficult to enlarge the notion of general intellect far beyond the kind of knowledge which is material-ized in fixed capital, to include also those forms of knowledge which structure social communications and which impel the activity of mass intellectual labour. . . . What we call mass intellectuality is living labour in its function as the determining articulation of the 'general intellect'.
>
> (Virno, 1996: 270)

The other side to Baudrillard's bleak vision of the masses themselves becoming a medium for the reproduction of capital is this: a general availability of a new productive resource, a General Intellect that, precisely because it is beyond the property of control of any single agent, or group of agents, lends itself to be employed within autonomous productive practices.

What then is the make up of this entirely socialized General Intellect? To Virno, it consists in a sociality liberated from the discipline of industrial society, to form the new and less hierarchical forms of interaction that have developed out of the counter-cultures of the 1960s and 1970s. These permit new, more flexible and nomadic forms of sociality that easily lend themselves to be deployed within post-Fordist production processes. Another, and to my mind equally obvious candidate is Media Culture. Even if the culture industries are privately owned, and even if access fees are charged for some content, like new feature films or video games and (decreasingly) music, most of Media Culture is generally and freely available. It has to be, since its value is based on the amount of attention that it can accumulate. This attention is in turn nothing but another term for its usefulness as a general resource in the marketing of consumer goods (either with a view to sales or to the creation of further attention to be realized as brand values). Contemporary marketing in its media-savvy way directly deploys the General Intellect of media culture as a productive power. (And given the common nature of this resource it is beyond value (cf. Negri, 1996)). The valorization of particular media products thus takes place through more or less artificial measurements of the attention (eyeballs or clicks) that it can generate (Smythe, 1980). But consumers also use Media Culture as a productive resource. They deploy the competences, the symbolic complexes, the signifying networks that have been established within Media Culture as a resource, a sort of language if you will, that can be used to perform the common that they produce in their agency. But Media Culture not only serves as a common resource. Its entering into the framework of social action also means that, like the machine in the factory, it *mediates social interaction differently* and makes new forms of productive co-operation possible. (Ghetto fashions enable disadvantaged youth from Norway to Brazil to produce music, style, community and eventually a political perspective together.) This way it is true, as both Adorno and McLuhan would agree, that the re-mediation of social life produced by its subsumption under capital in the form of media culture has put an end to the humanity of bourgeois, literary 'Man'. But at the same time a new kind of humanity – or productive communality (cf. Arendt, 1958) – has emerged. This way, 'advertising and pornography, the mourners that accompanied humanity to its grave, are also the innocent midwives of its new incarnation' (Agamben, 2001: 44).

The common availability of Media Culture as a General Intellect, and the new forms of productive co-operation that it makes possible, mean that the productivity of consumers tends to exceed the programming efforts of marketing. As the following chapters will show, it is this excess productivity that brand management seeks to appropriate.

Coda: mediatization and consumption

Branded goods are experiential commodities. At least according to the marketing literature, it is how they make you *Sense*, *Feel*, *Think*, *Act* and *Relate* (Schmitt, 1999), that makes up the core of their use-value. However, contrary to, say, a feature film, and like, say, a computer game, brands do not so much provide ready made experiences, as much as they enable the production, or co-creation, of an experience, or, for that matter, more enduring forms of immaterial use-values, like identity and community. Brands thus rely on the productivity of consumers not only for the realization, but for the actual co-production of the values that they promise. Like contemporary consumption more generally, brands depend on consumers rendering these objects part of themselves and of their life-world, on consumers letting themselves 'become part of the experience of being with products' (Firat and Dholakia, 1998: 97). This capacity on the part of consumers to become one with the brand is linked to the mediatization of consumption. Indeed, from the point of view of capital, the culture industries produce a kind of 'non-durable producers' goods' by putting the attention and affect of consumers to work. From this point of view, Media Culture works as a productive infrastructure that enables the creation and re-production of a valuable context of consumption (in excess of what is supplied by other interests, like the state apparatus). At the same time, consumers are known to use goods and Media Culture as tools to be employed in the everyday performance of identity, community, solidarity, emotional attachments and other immaterial use-values, in ways that are no longer directed by tradition or social structure in any simple or straightforward way. From the point of view of consumers, Media Culture works as a productive infrastructure that is put to work in the construction of a common social world.

People in all societies seem to have used goods – objects with one form of use-value or another – to represent or enact social relations. Anthropologists have been stressing this for a long time now. Marcel Mauss' (1954), Malinowski's (1932) and, more recently, Marilyn Strathern's (1988) work have all shown how the circulation of objects creates or underpins social relations in one manner or another. Mary Douglas and Brian Isherwood (1979) made the same claim for contemporary Western societies. They argued that consumer goods essentially work to give a tangible reality to 'culture' and the social relations that support it. Pierre Bourdieu (1984) too has showed how the correct use of goods works to maintain social divisions, that ultimately translate into differential endowments of real resources, like power, status and cultural and economic capital. Indeed, it seems close to a universal that, in Arjun Appadurai's words: 'the trajectories of things pattern human societies' (1986: 5). But, there is a generally recognized difference between the effects of modern goods and those of their non-modern counterpart. To put it a bit crudely, non-modern goods are used to reproduce existing forms of sociality, and modern goods are used to produce new forms of sociality. This is by no means an absolute difference: one can find instances of innovative consumption in non-modern societies, as much as one can find (many) instances of reproductive consumption in modern societies. But, tendentially:

> Modern consumers are the victims of the velocity of fashion as surely as primitive consumers are the victims of the stability of sumptuary law. From the point of view of demand, the critical difference between modern capitalist societies and those based on simpler forms of technology and labour is . . . that the consumption demands of persons in our own society are regulated by high turnover of criteria of appropriateness (fashion), in contrast to the less frequent shifts in more directly regulated sumptuary or customary systems.
>
> (Appadurai, 1986: 32)

In Appadurai's words, this is essentially *a difference in turn-over time*. And that difference can be attributable to the impact of mediatization.

The distinguishing element of modern consumer goods is that they are mediatized. Goods are connected to the intertextual web of meanings, symbols, images and discourses diffused by (mostly commercial) media like television, magazines, film, radio, the internet, and, most importantly perhaps, advertising – what I have called 'Media Culture'. What then does mediatization do?

One way to begin to answer that question is to give some precision to this increasingly popular concept (at least within Media Studies; cf. Schultz, 2004). To some extent all human communication is of course mediatized, at least to the extent that it makes use of a medium (be this spoken language or the language of gestures and bodily demeanour) that transforms or distorts the intended message of 'the sender'. Seen in this way, *communication* is not so much the matter of transmitting a message, as it is a matter of making something common, of producing something new and shared (Peters, 1999). Because people cannot understand each other directly, they have to produce an intelligible world that they can have in common. Insofar as this production of a *common* employs meaningful discourse, it necessarily produces a virtual double in retaining its own possibility of being different. Indeed, the particular feature of *meaning*, as brilliantly described by Niklas Luhmann (1990) is its ability to retain what has been negated as a possibility. Human communication thus necessarily produces a horizon of virtuality by implying that things, because they are as they are, could be different (cf. Levy, 1998: 170). This virtuality is real – it can have the power to affect social relations – although it is not actual: it is real in its potentiality. Media culture – by which we mean the culture of modern mass mediated communications – extends this horizon of virtuality by connecting diverse communication processes to each other and thus making them unfold within a common ambience.

Gabriel Tarde stressed this in his discovery of a new modern subjectivity, particular to the age of mass media, the public. In Tarde's version, the public consists in the connected rationality of individual minds, that hence come to act together. The public thus institutionalizes a collective production process, the outcomes of which – public opinion, 'truth', 'beauty' or 'utility' – are beyond the control of any single agent or class of agents (Tarde, 1901). Of course, certain members of a public can be more influential than others – Tarde distinguishes between innovative and repetitive forms of reception – but as a whole the public is an autonomous and socialized unit of immaterial production – of the production of virtuality (Lazzarato, 1997). This argument has since been developed by Jürgen Habermas (1989) who – without quoting Tarde – shows how the networking of communication in the bourgeois public sphere created an autonomous form of rationality that could act as a political force in its own right, irreducible to the will of a single individual or elite. (Remarkably, Habermas has then gone on to posit the mediatization of social communication in opposition to the autonomy of reason, even though he claims that the emergence of a media-networked bourgeois public was necessary for its emergence in the first place.) As is well known, the emergence of autonomous communication networks – publics – was a crucial factor behind the construction of real and influential virtualities like 'the Nation' (Anderson, 1991; Deutsch, 1953). Drawing on Tarde and (a somewhat unconventional reading of Habermas), we can thus think of media culture as a sort of network of publics. This makes the outcome of a socialized productivity available

for the single individual or small group. It provides a common meaningful horizon – a General Intellect – that can be employed as a productive
resource in particular instances of communication. The availability
of this resource serves both to empower the production of virtual, or
fantastic, alternatives to the present, and to provide a common horizon
that can unify the communication process in new ways, across
geographic and cultural boundaries, and make new forms of productive
co-operation possible.

Indeed, the supposed dangers of such enhanced fantasies have formed
an important rationale behind calls for the regulation of mass media –
from the dangers of subversive literature via the dangers of American
cinema to the recent hazards of violent video 'nasties' (that supposedly
cause young men to act out imaginary fist fights for real), and of
immersive computer games (that are supposed to cause addiction to
the fantasy worlds that they provide). Perhaps Durkheim's concept of
anomie can be read as pointing precisely at these intrinsically modern
dangers of an excessive, media-enhanced imagination. Durkheim defined
anomie as a situation in which one imagines forms of life for oneself that
go beyond what is realistically possible or socially permissible. He argued
that this occurs when the individual is suddenly put outside of the control
exercised by the implicit laws and expectations of the social, like rapid
social mobility (downwards but also upwards) and divorce. Durkheim
thought that the specifically modern nature of anomie was connected to
the mobility of modern life. But others, like Rosalind Williams (1982)
have argued that anomie as a particularly modern state of mind should
also be connected to the enhanced fantasy life that comes with mass
media and consumer culture. In other words anomie is not just a
consequence of a new social mobility (if there indeed was one), but also
of the fact that modern people live in a social environment where mass
media stimulate their imagination to the point of excess. Anomie is a
result of a new mobility of the imagination.

Historians have pointed at the connection between the extension of
publics, through new forms of mediated communication, and the spread
of consumer goods. Already Werner Sombart made this connection in his
Luxury and Capitalism (1967). He argued that the development of a
dynamic demand for luxury goods, which Sombart considered crucial to
the development of modern capitalism, developed around the institutions of the royal court. The court with its formalized interaction
worked not only as a source of new fashions and styles. Its centrality and
visibility also made it into a kind of proto-mediatic spectacle where new
goods, through their connection to particular, visible courtly practices or

personalities, could be given meanings that were generally recognized. However, as Chandra Mukerji (1983) has argued, it is the link to an emerging print culture that marks the first real step towards a consumer culture in the modern sense. Print, Mukerji argues, functioned to unify and generalize tastes at the same time as expanding capitalism unified commerce:

> Printed works spread through the trading system as commodities, bringing with them ideas and tastes that created bonds among Europeans from a variety of geographical regions and social strata. In this way, printing helped fashion cultural ties that paralleled the new economic ones, making, for instance, the material culture throughout Europe in the sixteenth and seventeenth centuries more cosmopolitan, at the same time that the economic system was becoming more international.
>
> (Mukerji, 1983: 12)

Indeed, it is through their connection to media culture that modern consumer goods acquire the horizon of virtuality that is the source of much of the utility that they have for consumers. This also goes for relatively anonymous mass produced objects like cigarettes and chewing gum, that now can acquire deep and complex meanings: through its associations to movies, sports (like baseball) and popular music, chewing gum became an integral element to the myth of the 'American dream' (Redclift, 2004), as smoked by movie stars like Marlene Dietrich and Humphrey Bogart, cigarettes came to represent an attractive and slightly challenging 'modernity' (Hilton, 2000). By thus being filled with meaning in media culture, consumer goods can enable their user to think him- or herself different. *By means of cigarettes* it becomes possible to imagine oneself on Marlene Dietrich, or to draw more freely on this ideal to enact a challenging, modern femininity (cf. de Grazia, 1992). Simmel (1905 [1997]) has famously argued that the connection between modern consumer goods and individuality has to do with the introduction of choice into what was previously a traditionally determined relation between objects and subjects. But one could add that this probably also has to do with the fact that mediatization *extends the capacities of objects themselves*. Not only does one now have a choice, but one has a choice between objects that tell different stories.

But goods are also material objects. As such they can give a tangible actuality to these virtual possibilities. Goods can become tangible embodiments of fantasy that have real effects insofar as they change the way everyday life is lived, or at least push in this direction. Italian sociologist Francesco Alberoni has a wonderful example of this, taken from his ethnographic study of women's relations to mass-produced underwear and night-gowns in Southern Italy in the early 1960s.

> To possess and use a modern [mass produced] night-gown carries a connotation of rebellion against the old austerity of the *corredo* [dowry]. It means to introduce motives that were previously rigorously excluded, to affirm, symbolically and implicitly one's own freedom to choose any man that one desires and to be desirable even after marriage. It carries the possibility of a fantastic, playful and sensual affective life that was unimaginable before. To buy such a night-gown not only radically weakens the very institution of dowry, but introduces the opportunity for choice in a context where the strength of that institution has derived from its traditional immutability. It carries a challenge to the traditional meaning of marriage, the traditional relation to the husband and to the children. It means to imagine a different kind of family, with different roles and new kinds of freedoms.
>
> (Alberoni, 1967: 39)

The modern night-gown connects to new fantasies of modernity. It can push one to live differently with others. Like mediatized consumer goods in general it is a means of production that can be deployed in the construction of a common social world.

3   Marketing

When [in 1960] I became director of design
at the Paris office of Raymond Loewy, *La
Compagnie de l'Esthetique Industrielle*, Industrial
Aesthetics – the cosmetic appearance of products – was
the core of what both practitioners and clients
assumed design was about. If, as often happened
along the way to figuring out how things should
look, we did some serious work on what people
wanted or how things worked, were used,
maintained and disposed of, well, that was nice,
but we did not get paid to do it. [Today] New Design is
almost an inversion of the old model. At the core today
is human-centered innovation.
(Arnold S. Wasserman, 'The New Design',
index magazine, 2004)

This paradigm shift described by an industrial designer is but one manifestation of a more general trend within managerial practice. Virtually all
of the discursive practices that, in an advanced economy mediate the
encounter between labour and capital – management, marketing, public
relations, ergonomics, design, advertising , and so on – have experienced
a similar shift. Until the 1960s, these were practices that worked against
the productivity of the social: Taylorist management sought to discipline
an unruly labour force into adopting certain pre-programmed forms of
behaviour; Public Relations was about propagating a certain corporate
ideology against public adversity to big business; marketing sought to
make consumers behave and desire in a certain way; and design was
about imposing more beautiful or rational objects on the recalcitrant
masses. Today, in almost every case, it is the other way around. Management now emphasizes *The Human Side of Enterprise* (to use the title of
Douglas McGregor's revolutionary 1960 pamphlet); the goal is to work

with the freedom of the employee, aligning his or her self-realization with the interests of the organization (Rose, 1999). Public Relations is less about imposing a certain vision or perspective than about moving with the public perception of the company, politician or a product, and putting a series of communicative processes to work by means of strategic tools like spinning, impression management and viral marketing, in order to organize the production of desirable forms of truth and opinion. Marketing, as this and the next two chapters will show, has developed from an overall attempt to impose what Jean Baudrillard (1970) called a 'code of value', to finding ways of working with consumers so that what they say or do can generate value. There has been an overall shift in the ways in which capital relates to (advanced forms of) labour.

Within these discourses themselves this shift is often described in terms of progress and improvement. Management has become less 'hierarchical' and more 'democratic', more open to the actual needs and desires of employees. Marketing has becomes less 'bureaucratic' and more 'humanistic' – better in touch with what people actually want and crave, 'more true to people's real life' to use the words of British marketing guru John Grant (1999: xiii). From certain particular viewpoints it is of course possible to make such value judgements. What is often forgotten, however, is that this 'humanistic turn' in managerial discourse (to use a common term) has been premised on a vast extension of the quality and quantity of information available to these practices. With this in mind, one can argue that the interest in human agency – in cultural practice – on the part of marketing has been a consequence of the availability of new kinds of information that allows the subsumption of these kinds of practices as a source of surplus value. Managerial humanism thus enables a more far-reaching subsumption of human practice.

This chapter will describe how the informational reach of marketing has expanded as a parallel to the process of mediatization of consumption described in the previous chapter. The decisive event was the 'cultural turn' that marketing went through in the late 1950s and 1960s. This 'turn' was triggered by the emergence of the new forms of consumer agency that Chapter 2 attributed to the impact of electronic media. The new agency and creativity that consumers exposed made their behaviour less predictable. This, in turn created a demand for new research methodologies that could produce qualitative data on the cultural dimensions of consumption, as well as new theories that allowed the processing of such qualitative information. This qualitative expansion of the informational reach of marketing has been crucial to the development of brand management in the contemporary sense of the term.

Marketing can be understood as the management of the means of consumption. With management we understand a discursive practice that seeks to ensure that the means of production are used in a rational way. In the case of a capitalist economy this means making sure that, in Marx's words, the 'labour process becomes the instrument of the valorization process' (1990[1867]: 1019); to ensure that the means of production are used in such ways that generate surplus value. This entails creating an environment in which capital and labour can meet under organized forms: under such conditions that limit the range of options, and that make certain kinds of action more likely than others. In the case of management this means building and organization. In the case of marketing it entails constructing a market. As recent economic sociology has stressed, markets should not be taken as given or naturally occurring, but rather as the outcome of a complex array of institutional determinations, many guided by the very disciplines that propose to give an objective description of how markets work, like economics (Callon, 1998; Carrier and Miller, 1998). To 'make a market' means making the world of consumers and the world of business meet. In order for that to happen two conditions must be met. First, goods need to be inscribed into (or 'entangled' into) the life-world of consumers. They need to present themselves as objects that make sense and that can be used with relative ease. Second, the complexity of consumer practices needs to be reduced so that production can be programmed and consumer agency valorized. Marketing is the management of this complex array of choices and decisions. As in the case of management, this practice presupposes information. (Maybe even more than in the case of management as 'the market' tends to be less limited to a single physical place than 'the organization'.) Information provides an interface on which marketing can act. It constitutes its object – the consumer. As Don Slater (2002) has stressed, marketing is exercised on the arena of information. Marketing and advertising

> require deep cultural knowledges of the objectified other. It is not necessarily empirically correct knowledge (advertisers may be wrong, and infamously can never really know when they are wrong), but it must be knowledge that makes sense to the marketers as a cultural embedding of the product and, which therefore makes sense as a strategy for marketing.
>
> (Slater, 2002: 247)

It follows that transformations in the informational interface of marketing also mean transformations in its managerial reach. New forms of information allow the subsumption of new kinds of practices. This chapter will describe the development of the informational interface of marketing during the twentieth century. I build my case chiefly around the history of American marketing. Although there are of course national and regional differences, this remains a legitimate practice, at least for the post-war years. In terms of methods of information gathering and theories of consumer behaviour – the informational interface of marketing – what national differences that might have prevailed in the pre-war years, rapidly disappear after the Second World War, when American methods became the global norm (cf. Arvidsson, 2003).

Marketing: the early developments

Although advertising and salesmanship have a long history, marketing in the modern sense is distinctive. It constitutes a discourse informed by coherent methods, models and forms of knowledge. As a coherent discursive practice, modern marketing first developed in the United States in the early twentieth century, as academics in the new business schools began to give serious consideration to the problem of distribution (Bartels, 1976; Fullerton, 1988). This had become a pertinent issue as mass production, mass transport and, importantly, mass communications had opened up the possibility of constructing national markets governed by common taste and preference systems (Tedlow, 1990; Levi Martin, 1999). Inspired by German institutional economics, early academic marketing thought was mainly concerned with the institutional framework of commercial distribution, with markets, middlemen and transportation systems. Interest in consumer behaviour rather developed within the field of advertising psychology. There the pioneering work of Walter Dill Scott (1903) had established a view of consumers as weak and open to persuasion through the suggestive effects of advertising. (This view was coherent with major European psychological traditions, like the 'Psychology of Suggestion' adapted to advertising theory by the two French psychologists Octave Jacques Gérin and Charles Éspinadel in their *La publicité suggestive* (1911), a work that Scott prefaced cf. Arvidsson, 2001; Nye, 1975.) This view was later developed by the famous behaviourist, James W. Watson, who had been hired by the J. Walter Thompson advertising agency in 1920. He argued that the systematic use of strong emotional appeals, like 'fear, rage and love' could foster new forms of overall consumer behaviour, regardless of the individual situation of consumers. Indeed, Watson claimed (again in tune with the times) that 'we act and think as masses', and as masses people could easily be educated to, in his co-worker Helen Resor's words: 'accept, desire and demand the things that are part of the increased standard of living' (Kreshel, 1989: 177).

This view of human subjectivity as formable and open to environmental influences made early advertising psychology work well with the overall disciplinary project of Taylorism. There were many points of contact and agreement between 'Taylorist' managers and engineers and marketers and advertising psychologists. Both disciplines were part of a capitalist 'control revolution' (Beniger, 1986) driven by the new productive powers unleashed by industrialization and made possible by new administrative (the telephone, the typewriter) and persuasive (advertising, the weekly press) media. Here, the government of consumption was seen as a necessary parallel to the government of production. With good reason, Henry Ford is often mentioned as a pioneer of this new concern with organizing consumption (and 'Fordism' has come to signify a system based on mass production for mass consumption). It is often remembered that Ford stressed the importance of higher wages that would enable workers to purchase the products that they produced. Of equal importance to this Keynesian insight however is the fact that Ford was deeply concerned with educating workers and shaping their consumer behaviour. It was not just important that workers consumed, but also how they consumed. Accordingly, Ford's plant in Highland Park had a social science division, social workers visited worker homes, housewives were taught Home Economics and 'wholesome' forms of consumption like gardening and various forms of hobbies were encouraged, while 'unwholesome' forms like the consumption of alcohol and the associated unstructured (or promiscuous) sociality were discouraged. Indeed, in the original definition of Fordism by the Italian Marxist thinker Antonio Gramsci (1971), the stress is not only on the principle of high wages and proletarian consumerism, but also on the importance of control of consumption and, by extension, of private life in general. Gramsci lists the prohibition movement, sexual puritanism and organizations like the YMCA and Rotary as important components of the new planned economy organized around the factory. Within early marketing thought there was a similar emphasis on re-education; on replacing particular, private, ethnic or class-specific tastes and consumer practices with modern, rational and distinctively middle class ones.

Despite its ambitious goal to be part of an overall reorganization of society (Ewen, 1976; Lears, 1994), early marketing thought developed with very little empirical knowledge about consumers. In part this was deemed unnecessary since the persuasive effects of advertising would in any case over-ride individual habits and attachments. In part this was because the necessary survey methods had not yet been developed. In the first post-war years, however, the advances of empirical psychological research and the emergence of readership surveys began to supply such information. As the development of market and audience research accelerated, in particular in the wake of the depression, the nature of marketing changed. In the 1930s, Laufer and Paradeise claim in their history of marketing and public opinion research, marketing became 'less about shaping consumer demand and more about finding out what and why people want' (1990: 52). It is important however not to interpret these events naïvely. It is true, on the one hand, that marketers now had more data about consumers on their hands and that this new data was put to use in developing advertising that represented consumers in their 'real' habitat, presenting products as responses to what was thought to be their real needs. The new availability of data was also paralleled by an increasing emphasis on the importance of advertising realism. It is not so clear, on the other hand, whether this realism actually mirrored the actual lived reality of consumers. Indeed, one could argue, that realism in advertising was more of a conventional than of a representational kind. To clarify this it is necessary to examine the post-war development of advertising and market research in more detail.

Realism in advertising

The production of sociological, and not just psychological knowledge about consumers – knowledge about their tastes, habits and preferences – was driven by the publishing industry. For the new mass circulating weekly and monthly magazines that often retailed at less than production costs and thus relied heavily on advertising, it was particularly important to procure additional information that could define and valorize their audience in the eyes of advertisers. (Daily newspapers felt this problem less, as their market was in most cases given by geographical factors; Wernick, 1991.) Indeed this kind of marketing was undertaken even before adequate methods for producing the necessary knowledge were available. Already in the 1890s mass circulating magazines like *Ladies World* made use of letters to the editor and photographs of subscribers' homes to imply that their readership was representative of a particular kind of households with a particular outlook, taste and consumer habits, a particular 'habitus' for short. Thus *Harpers' Bazaar* was supposedly read in upper class households, *Ladies Home Journal* represented an audience of rational and frugal middle class housewives, and so on (Ohmann, 1996; Fox, 1984; Scanlon, 1995). In the immediate post-war years, however, big publishers like Curtis (*True Story, Love Magazine, Ladies Home Journal*) set up research departments, and a number of research consultancies, like the Eastman company, developed to service small publishers (in the case of Eastman the *Christian Herald* and *Cosmopolitan* magazine). All of these surveyed readers for data on income and demographic composition (Lockley, 1950). In the 1930s it became common for mass circulating magazines (and for radio companies like CBS) to maintain reader's panels. *Woman's Home Companion*, for example, launched a panel in 1935, consisting first of 250 and then expanding to 1,500. Panellists were selected to represent different ages, occupations and income levels among the journal's readers, and they were asked to answer a survey on matters such as family size, husband's occupation, type and size of home, furniture, equipment, gardens, domestic help, laundry methods, car ownership, income levels, interests and hobbies. On the panel, members were frequently interviewed on topics like 'meal planning, food preparation, laundry fashions, household equipment, leisure time, home decoration, and child care'. The CBS panel was checked in even more detail. Through so called 'pantry checks' an interviewer visited the homes of housewives on the panel over a period of several weeks to observe which brand names had appeared and disappeared (Converse, 1987: 92, ff.; Lazarsfeldt, 1938). Much data on consumer demographics, behaviour and purchasing patterns was thus generated. However, information on the cultural framework of consumer practice, on the ideas, values and motivations that lay behind people's choice and actions, was blatantly absent. Concomitant with the background assumptions of both Taylorism and Watson's behaviourism, it was actions, not ideas that counted: market research registered what consumers did, not why they did it. To some extent this omission was motivated by certain pre-conceived ideas about what counted as knowledge, by assumptions at the level of what Foucault (1972) called *savoir*. But there was no real pressure to procure such knowledge. Indeed, consumer motivations, and hence the kinds of arguments that could be efficiently employed in advertisements were thought to be readily deductible from the cultural environment, or life-world, embodied by a particular magazine. As the Spanish American Publishing company claimed in an advertisement for *Cinelandia*, a motion picture magazine directed to the Latin American market: 'just a glance through the magazine shows you the type to whom it is directed' (*Export Advertiser*, 1930). Media like weekly magazines and cinema supplied a format, a set of arguments and cultural backdrop for advertising. The developments of the J. Walter Thompson Lux account testify to this mechanism. The account was taken on in 1916, and Lux soap was originally marketed as an upscale product, suitable to wash fashion garments (JWT, 1935a). In 1922 it was decided to sell the soap in the form of flakes, suggesting a more everyday use to a wider market (JWT, 1935b). This led to a series of advertisements depicting the product in the context of an (imaginary) middle class life, deploying the graphic style of upscale women's magazines, like *Cosmopolitan*, *Women's Home Companion*, and *Ladies Home Journal*. According to Stanley Resor, head of JWT, the use of personal testimonials and intimate confessions was a direct response to the focus on personal matters and human interest that prevailed in the magazines: he thought he knew, from reading women's magazines that housewives were easily swayed by 'personal appeal and human interest, hence such forms of address should be used in advertising as well' (JWT, 1928). When tabloids and confession magazines like *True Story* gained momentum, and when advertising agencies began considering them legitimate outlets for advertising in the late 1920s ('after a short cultural lag', Marchand, 1985: 56), this personal format was retained, but set in humbler social circumstances, that were supposedly representative of the life-world of the lower class readers of these publications. As the content of the 'true stories' of these publications tended to stress *social* failure (or success), advertising also stressed the theme of 'social ostracism', emphasizing how products could save their users from the catastrophic social consequences of 'dishpan hands' or 'undie odour'. With the arrival of photography and the comic format in the 1930s (considered highly efficient because of its realistic appeal), this theme was further developed. It is interesting to note that the only research into consumer motivations undertaken by J. Walter Thompson regarded the particular *activities* that women found interesting. It emerged that the target audience (middle and lower class women) was most interested in washing stockings and in the consequences of soap on hands. These two activities became the focus of the campaign. The way that they were framed, however, was entirely given by the mediatic environment (JWT, 1929). Advertising employed realistic conventions borrowed from the women's magazines, just as market research employed a *conventional understanding* of class-based consumer cultures as a backdrop to its production of knowledge.

Copywriters and advertising theorists kept stressing that advertising should give realistic representations of the life of consumers, provide situations, or as Roland Marchand (1985) has called them, 'Social

Tableaux' in which consumers could recognize themselves. But they had very few means of knowing the meaningful make-up of that reality. True, they had a lot of data on activities, on choices, uses and purchases, but virtually none on the motivations and attachments. Instead, the meaningful reality that advertising represented, its concerns, fears and desires, emerged through the interface of women's magazines. Realistic advertising, or 'capitalist realism' as Schudson (1984) famously called it, was thus not so much a representation of the actual lived reality of consumers as much as it was a convention, a genre. Indeed, a conventional reality served as a substitute for the kinds of information that was not available. For the advertisers, adopting the conventional realism of the weekly magazines became a way to black box the issue of consumer motivations. This was particularly clear in the case of the influential ABCD typology that has come to guide market research up until the present day.

One key characteristic of the conventional 'reality' adopted by marketing was the supposition that structures of needs and desires were tied to income. This link was further strengthened when radio promoted the development of nation-wide ratings research in the 1930s. Now class differences roughly coinciding with differences between magazines were reified into a standardized typology, the so-called ABCD system. As we can see from the way the J. Walter Thompson Corporation's chief researcher Paul Cherington (1924) recommended the operationalization of the ABCD system, income differences were understood to imply a lot more about life-styles and outlook. To him the categories meant the following:

A. Homes of substantial wealth above the average in culture that have at least one servant. The essential point, however, in this class is that the persons interviewed shall be people of intelligence and discrimination.
B. Comfortable middle class homes, personally directed by intelligent women.
C. Industrial homes of skilled mechanics, mill operators or petty trades people (no servants).
D. Homes of unskilled labourers or in foreign districts where it is difficult for American ways to penetrate.

(Cherington, 1924)

There were no research data on motivations and attitudes that could substantiate such descriptions. (Nobody ever tested for 'intelligence and discrimination', for example.). Rather, the ABCD typology worked as a way of giving 'scientific' legitimacy to speculations about aspects of consumer behaviour on which there were no data available. Indeed, as the ABCD typology was sedimented in the 1930s through its deployment in the Cooperative Analysis of Broadcasting's (CAB) nation-wide ratings research (which became the standard measure in the 1930s), and latter in the Nielsen ratings index (launched in 1942), it provided a convenient ground for such speculations. Indeed, in the CAB survey much was hypothesized (or, 'surmised' to use the actual expression) about the actual behaviour of each group. The relatively small share of the radio audience pertaining to group A was supposed to be explained not only by economic factors but also by 'them having . . . a wide range of social interests and activities limiting time for listening [and] the fact that the average program is directed to lower income groups making them of little interest for the A group'. Conversely, the C group's high index of listening was explained by 'lower educational standards' making listening the 'preferable way of getting information' (Beville, 1940; 198, ff.; James, 1937; cf. Bogart, 1987). As the ABCD typology was sedimented as the main basis for market and audience 'nose counting', it came to work as a convenient sorting device. It permitted market and audience researchers to place consumers (and listeners) in established categories based on data on income and/or residence. Once placed in such a category accompanying assumptions about relatively fixed motivations, attitudes and life-styles made it possible to legitimately deduce further ideas about consumers, and how to appeal to them. This way, the ABCD typology worked to reduce, or contain the complexity of consumer motivations into a relatively neat and simple typology that permitted a highly standardized and streamlined marketing effort. With the ABCD typology classifications originally derived from the structure of the magazine advertising market were developed into general categories, used to contain and manage a wide diversity of consumer practices. The ABCD typology became the very foundation for the construction of a Baudrillardian code of consumption, intended to contain the productivity of the social.

In the inter-war years, advertising took a realist direction. It pretended to represent people in their everyday environment and to provide arguments that 'made sense' in relation to their everyday concerns. Rather than any serious attempt to actually represent the lived reality of consumers, this realism emerged out of a series of conventions that had developed, mainly, around the market for audiences for weekly magazines. Audience research provided marketers with a number of categories that could be used to differentiate between consumer goods. As these categories were sedimented into a commonly used typology they also came to provide a common-sense ground for deducting ideas about consumer motivations and attitudes from income. Similarly, the layout of weekly magazines and their discursive content supplied advertisers with a number of arguments and stylistic conventions to be deployed in producing 'realistic' representations of consumer life-worlds. Here too, these conventions sedimented over time, into a set of common-sense assumptions as to how the life of consumers actually looked. The nexus between advertising and the weekly magazines came to construct a 'Reality' (or perhaps better, a 'real virtuality') to which advertising could refer in making claims about products, and marketing could use in managing the contact between consumers, goods and the means of consumption. For the advertising professionals, this real virtuality served as a substitute for the kinds of information that could not yet be produced. For the consumers, it served as a visualization of the prevailing consumption norm and helped establish the truth, beauty and utility of products.

The cultural turn

Chapter 2 described a series of factors that combined to transform American middle class consumer culture in the 1950s and 1960s: suburbanization, the recomposition of the middle classes themselves, the counter-culture, the impact of television and of new objects and environments of consumption, like plastic, frozen foods, the supermarket and the shopping mall. Even if these developments produced new practices that fell outside of the reality captured by the conventions of advertising, they were by no means ignored by marketing professionals, at least not by the vanguards of the advertising and marketing profession. To these 'organic intellectuals', the traditional 'realistic' advertising genre was losing its efficiency: people were becoming less prone to identify with the reality that it depicted. While changes in consumer culture were important in provoking these transformations, new factors within the business world itself also played their part. Industrial over-capacity produced a higher pressure for product differentiation (Smith, 1956; Keith, 1960; Tedlow, 1990). Combined with new developments in design and in shopping environments, this led to a growing pressure to differentiate product lines to target different consumer segments (or to invent new products altogether as in the tobacco and automobile industries). Combined with the sociological changes described in Chapter 2, this introduced new amounts of 'stuff' into the middle class life-world, which in turn enabled new kinds of consumer practices. The most important factor behind the growing 'crisis' of advertising in the 1960s however, was the availability of more and new kinds of information. In 1963 the turnover of the research business was ten times (in current dollars) that of thirty years before. With the expansion of the research community came its professionalization. More trained social scientists were employed and theories and methods refined (Bogart, 1963; cf. Rainwater *et al.*, 1959). The result was a pressure to generate more detailed and deeper descriptions of consumer behaviour and a growing suspicion towards the fixed categories implied by the ABCD system. In combination with the emerging new forms of consumer agency, or 'mass intellectuality' described in Chapter 2, consumer behaviour now seemed much less predictable than before.

Within the world of advertising, a number of 'new prophets' emerged to call for a reform of the ways in which advertising depicted consumers, goods and their relations. While there were sometimes profound disagreements among these as to what was to be done, all agreed that the older, well-established realist format no longer worked. They argued that advertising now met with a chronic attention deficit. (This discovery owed a lot to the new kinds of information that was now available from large-scale, nation-wide measurements of advertising recall and of the influence of advertising on purchases.) In a more diversified and rich media environment, advertising was only one voice, and not a particularly influential one. As Bill Bernbach, a central figure of the New York based 'creative revolution' in advertising put it in a 1965 interview:

> We wondered whether the advertising community was loved by the American people. We're not even hated! They ignore us. So the most important thing as far as I'm concerned is to be fresh, to be original – to be able to compete with all the shocking news events in the world today, with all the violence. Because you can have all the right things in an ad, and if nobody is made to stop and listen to you, you've wasted it.
>
> (Higgins, 1965: 14)

Most also agreed that the reason for this lack of interest in advertising was that people generally felt that advertisements did not speak of things that interested them, or even of things that made sense. Advertisements tended to use difficult or technical terminology that was incomprehensible to most people. They were written by middle class academics, for middle class academics, and their verbose language simply escaped most common people. Indeed, their reliance on a 'wordy' style squared badly with an emerging visual mentality fostered by electronic media.

> [A]s a middle class, well educated group, advertising people naturally assume that all Americans are involved with words on the same levels that they are. But in point of truth, relatively few human beings are actually skilled with words. Brought up on an intellectual diet of Grade B movies, comic books, sports pages, and electronic comedians, the average individual is not equipped to cope with the professional communicator.
>
> (Martineau, 1957: 1)

Rosser Reeves, another famous 'advertising prophet' disagreed vehemently with this point. He agreed however, that most people found little interest in advertising. The reason he proposed was that most advertisements consisted of empty claims that said very little about the product and the potential benefits that the consumer could derive from it. Reeves (1961) proposed more 'Reality' in advertising, or, claims about tangible product attributes that actually made a difference to the consumer, and that he or she could empirically verify. Martineau, on the other hand, called for advertisements that stimulated a greater emotional involvement on the part of consumers. While their recipes were different, the core of the advice was the same. Advertising must engage consumers; it must trigger some sort of mental activity with them; it must activate or engage them in some sense. It was no longer enough to inscribe the product in a well-established Reality, and then suppose that this, in itself would trigger actual purchases. (These ideas were supported by the development of new research techniques, like Motivation Research – of which Martineau was a pioneer and Reeves a vehement enemy – that uncovered new levels of consumer agency; see below.) Finally, all agreed on the necessity to streamline and concentrate the advertising message. Rooser Reeves made this the core of his philosophy, championing the USP (Unique Selling Proposition) as the core of every campaign. In his words: 'The consumer tends to remember just one thing from an advertisement – one strong claim, or one strong concept' (Reeves, 1961: 34). All of this tended to introduce a sharper focus on the product, or rather the way in which it figured in advertising. This principle was perhaps driven furthest by the new creative agencies, like Collett, Dickenson & Pearce (CDP) in London, and Doyle, Dane & Bernbach (DDB) in New York, who would set the pace for much of 1960s advertising. For both agencies, an increasing focus on the advertising message and the feeling, mode or experience that it could convey constituted an alternative to and a reaction against the increasing recourse to 'science' (meaning quantitative data) that mainstream agencies engaged in as a response to a more complex environment. Instead of trying to keep track of consumer reactions through 'scientific' research, Bernbach emphasized the importance of the ad's enduring emotional impact. Bernbach also broke with the realist ethos that had been central to modern advertising. He emphasized that the point of advertising was not to represent consumer wants and desires but to position and give personality to *products*. Advertising served first to interpret the product, rather than the consumer: 'to find the simple story in the product and present it in an articulate, intelligent and persuasive way'. Furthermore, Bernbach's advertising was reflexive, rather than realist: it commented on advertising and frequently mocked its conventions. This was evident, for example, in his famous Volkswagen commercials that mocked the established conventions of automobile advertising. In 1963 DDB even ran an ad with no picture or headline, just a series of instructions for 'How to do a Volkswagen ad'. To Bernbach, as to his followers in the 'creative revolution' advertising had lost its innocence as a representational medium. It had become one of many genres in an increasingly interlinked media culture. A good advertisement would not so much seek to provide consumers with an ideal that they could identify with, but to give identity to a product by linking it to the intertextual universe of media culture of which advertising itself was a part. In London, Stanley Pollitt, of the Boase, Massimi & Pollitt (BMP) agency, thought in similar terms. He argued (against the 'scientist' approach) that however complex, statistical models offered a too simplistic view of how advertising influenced consumers. This was particularly true in a highly differentiated and complex media environment where consumers were constantly confronted with different atmospheres and life-styles. More importantly perhaps, he claimed that consumers perceived advertising, the brand and its media environment as a totality. To try to break this down to measurable parts, as quantitative methods necessarily had to do, might produce dangerous and misleading results. Instead, it was important to focus on what he called the brand image, on the symbolic totality of the product's mediatic presentation. Although Pollitt was not first to point at the importance of brand image (Burleigh Gardner and Sydney Levy had used this term already in 1955; see below), he added a new, holistic dimension to the term. Brand image was to be understood as something above and beyond the perceptions of individual consumers. While these still mattered, the creation and maintenance of successful brand images was chiefly a matter of artistic creativity. The 1960s thus saw a revival of 'art' against 'science' in advertising. (These two conceptions of the trade had been fighting it out since the beginning of modern advertising.) Through the creative revolution this artistic revival was temporarily connected to the counter-cultural critique of mass society, a lot of its style and imagery was incorporated into advertising. In many ways, these debates constituted a first step in shifting the focus away from the (pre-given) Reality of advertising, and towards the productive potential of particular products: the mood, feeling or experience that they could stimulate in consumers.

Although the growing emphasis on 'image' and 'feeling' that marked the vanguard of the advertising industry in the 1960s was often framed in terms of a return of 'art' against 'science', this was not the whole story. The new emphasis on the cultural and experiential dimensions of goods was also a reaction to the new conditions posed by the media environment. With the growing popularity of the concept of the 'brand image' came a new understanding of the unstable and 'contested' meaning of commodities within an ever more complex media environment, and of the productive and unpredictable nature of consumer practice. In an influential article, Sydney Levy and Burleigh Gardner claimed that people were now no longer naturally accepting of an older hierarchy of needs and motivations. They did not so much follow '(a) the striving to be economical or (b) the desire to emulate people of higher status' (Gardner and Levy, 1955: 34). What mattered now, more than before, was the symbolic dimension of the product, the 'brand image'. The brand image, Levy and Gardner argued, represents 'a public image, a character or personality that may be more important for the over-all status (and sales) of the brand than many technical facts about the product' (1955: 35). The brand results from the product's existence as a complex 'public object', 'it is made up of the meanings that advertising, merchandising, promotion, publicity, and even sheer length of existence have created'. Marketing thus had to work on this symbolic level, creating distinct 'brand images' or 'brand personalities' by means of advertising and other forms of mediated communication. Without such symbolic distinctions, '[h]ow else can they [consumers] decide whether to smoke Camels or Lucky Strikes; to use Nescafe or Borden's instant coffee; to drive a Ford or a Chevrolet or a Plymouth' (ibid.). As Sydney Levy summarized this in a subsequent article:

> Grandmother cherished her furniture for its sensible, practical value, but today people know that it is hardly the practical considerations which determine their choices between Post's and Kellogg's, Camels and Luckies, Oldsmobiles and Buicks, or Arpege and Channel No 5.

They know that package color, television commercials, and newspaper and magazine advertisements incline them towards one preference or another.

(Levy, 1964: 140)

Gardner and Levy's opposition between an earlier 'materialistic' or 'rationalistic' past and a symbolic-expressive present is as misleading as it is common among advertising and marketing writers. (And they were writing in a time where the marketing profession was heavily influenced by motivation psychology and its theory of an epochal shift from the material to the symbolic age; see below.) Advertising in the 1920s had of course also been highly 'symbolic' in nature, but then, its arguments had referred back to a given symbolic Reality. Now, however, the symbolic dimension of marketing practice was underlined as the public meaning of commodities was perceived to be less stable and their media environment more complex. Marketing had to think symbolically in order to navigate the emerging new more dynamic and complex Media Culture. This perception of a new contingency in the relations between consumers and products was strengthened by developments in market research.

The transformation of market research

The most important factor behind the transformation of market research in the 1960s was the transformation of the media environment. After all the largest consumers of market research were still media companies who sought to valorize their audiences in the eyes of advertising buyers. The main factor was the weekly and monthly press that responded to the rise of television as a mass advertising medium by marketing their audiences as representative of particular niches, styles or 'moods' (Broadbent, 1967). This 'decline of the mass media' and the rise of a more differentiated environment was a direct response to the new and more heterogeneous consumer practices (Maiser, 1973). The consequence of this development was that 'demographics' – meaning the particular demographic categories implied by the ABCD typology – no longer seemed to be a reliable guide to consumer segmentation (Bogart, 1966; Barnett, 1969; Yankelovich, 1964). One might know one's demographics, one speaker at British advertising journal *Admap*'s symposium for media executives in 1966 argued, but one could no longer be sure of how a particular demographic segment would respond to advertising (Admap, 1966).

The particular *response* that this triggered was, however, conditioned by the intellectual environment of marketing of the late 1950s and early

1960s. Marketing did not escape the heavy influence that psychoanalysis and, in particular, ego psychology exercised on American society in general at this time. Maslow's *Motivation and Personality* (1954) would have an important influence on marketing all through the 1960s (and it still does!). Maslow's idea of a historical progression along the 'hierarchy of needs' suggested that a post-materialistic, expressive age would follow on a materialistic, utilitarian recent past. To marketing's organic intellectuals this seemed plausible and in tune with the ongoing differentiation and becoming productive of consumer practice. It was however a new form of market research, Motivation Research, that supplied the strongest arguments for stressing the cultural function of goods. Pioneered by Austrian emigré psychoanalyst Ernest Dichter and Chicago based market researcher Pierre Martineau, Motivation Research was presented as an appropriate response to the dissolution of old consumption norms. Pierre Martineau argued, that during his recent experience as head of research of the *Chicago Tribune*, he had experienced 'a greater transformation in our system of values since 1940 than in the latest 2000 years of existence' (Martineau, 1957: 157). Americans in general were becoming middle class, he claimed, class mattered less and less, and as middle class, they were no longer so much interested in status achievement as in individual self-expression. Small, insignificant, everyday consumer decisions thus came to function as a vehicle for the expression of this new-found desire for individuality:

> As the gap between top and bottom extremes of wealth has been narrowed down it is no longer possible to be different merely by exhibiting an automobile, a college education for one's children, a Florida vacation or a home in the suburbs. But we can be different in our tastes. This is the avenue for individuation. Broadly we are all conformists: we are not going to be driving scooters or go barefoot to be different. But, within the limits of conformity we can develop individualistic styles in all areas of consumer wants to show our colourful, interesting personalities through our tastes. We look for pastel telephones, new models and new decors in our cars – some different beauty in any product, a certain luxury, a feature that can not be talked about. The wish for attention that might be repressed in hard times is in full bloom today.
>
> (Martineau, 1957: 159)

Ernest Dichter, shared this vision of a coming age of self-expression: in his 1965 *Harvard Business Review* article, entitled 'Discovering the inner Joneses', he argued that American (middle class) consumers' culture were moving in the direction of a new aesthetic 'to please the inner man'. The old, socially anchored logic of consumption was definitely out: '"What will the neighbours say?" may become an obsolete phrase within the near future.' The new standards were rather set by internal ideals, by 'the inner Joneses' who asked 'not how long will the washer last but what will it do for his soul'. This new standard of self-realization, Dichter argued, was also on its way to becoming a new criterion of distinction: 'The person who more truly becomes himself will be the one admired by the new "Joneses"' (Dichter, 1965: 157).

In order to strengthen and help diffusing this new consumer ethic, which both Dichter and Martineau considered more rational and evolved, marketing had to do its part. (Dichter linked this pursuit to higher ends: the struggle against communism. 'We are', he argued, 'in the midst of a silent war' against two enemies, the connection between which he leaves open: 'on the outside with Russia and on the inside with our old concepts of thinking'; Dichter: 1960: 16.) In order to win this two-sided war, it was necessary to rethink the relation between people and goods. Above all, marketing had to abandon the idea that consumers made rational decisions in relation to a socially given hierarchy of needs or values. Rather, in this new area of self-expression human desire was best regarded as plastic and open. Indeed people lived in a world of goods to which they were emotionally attached and to which they owed large parts of their own personality (although few would recognize this debt). It was to these unrecognized, irrational, emotional bonds that progressive market researchers now had to turn. In an early article from 1949 he concluded that, up until now, most advertisements made virtually identical claims.

> There is no toilet soap that will not give the user lovelier skin, no face cream that will not secure romance and eternal love for the purchaser, and no whiskey that is not milder, smoother, and longer aged than others on the market. It is small wonder that the reader has great difficulty in distinguishing one brand from another. It would be far more efficient to use advertising to give products a tangible experiential component.
>
> (Dichter, 1949)

Dichter then proceeded to suggest a better way. A psychological study showed the 'voluptuous' nature of ice cream to be one of its main appeals. In talking about ice cream, people commented: 'You feel you can drown yourself in it' and 'You want to get your whole mouth in it'. Similarly, although most deodorant advertising stressed the function of the product in guaranteeing 'social acceptance and safety', what really interests (women) deodorant users is 'to be able to like themselves, to feel clean to consider themselves smart beauty technicians' (Dichter 1949: 63). Similarly furniture was used to 'put into practice an emerging – even if unformulated – philosophy of life', and domestic appliances worked to 'create the home as part of yourself' (*Motivations*, 1956a); cigarettes were instruments deployed to 'cope with life' and shopping was a constitutive experience in the construction of the suburban couple's way of life (*Motivations*, 1956b, 1957). Motivation research thus began to argue that consumer choices should not be seen as a consequence of the consumers' innate wants and preferences (themselves a consequence of his or her position along the ABCD typology). Rather, consumption should be understood as a constructive practice by means of which the consumer produces his or her self, through more or less intimate liaisons with different products. As Sydney Levy (active as a Motivation Researcher) would write in an influential article on 'Symbolism and Life Style': 'a consumer's personality can be seen as the peculiar total of the products he consumes' (Levy, 1964: 149). Motivation research thus suggested that marketing take as its object the *programming* of this consumerist self-production. This naturally shifted the attention away from the innate or socially given qualities that a product already had (in relation to the established 'code of value'), towards the potential qualities or experiences that could be created for the product in relation to a particular consumer category. We need, Martineau claimed, 'to go beyond product claims and create an attractive mode or feeling in the form of a product or brand image' (1957: 5). This fundamental step, from the product to the relations between products and consumers (or better, the recognition of the contingency of these relations) constituted a first important step towards the contemporary branding paradigm (see below).

Motivation research also had a significant impact on quantitative market research. Out of the new openness to the multidimensionality of consumer motivations that it had fostered came what would later be known as psychographics (Demby, 1974). At the same time as motivation research had opened up the possibility of viewing consumer subjectivity as something that consumers produced, and not just something that was given by social structure, it was not methodologically capable of supplying valid and reliable information. Such methodological innovations came out of the work of the influential Chicago research company Social Research Incorporated (SRI). Like Paul

Lazarsfeldt's Bureau of Social Research, SRI was a place where market researchers and sociologists interacted. The methodological tools it developed were employed in the emerging field of sociological studies of class, like W. Lloyd Warner's *Yankee City* (1949) study, as well as in market research. Both sociologists and market researchers shared an interest in reliable quantitative instruments that could provide a picture of what was understood to be a changing American class landscape. In particular it became imperative to understand the culture of the 'class-less' middle classes, the 'White Collars' as C. Wright Mills would later describe them, who were understood to be de-linked from traditional ethnic or geographically rooted communities and appeared to form a kind of free floating mysterious entity (Mills, 1951; Whyte, 1955). In 1959 SRI sociologists Lee Rainwater, Richard Coleman and Gerald Handel published what has become know as the first life-style study, *The Workingman's Wife: Her Personality, World and Life Style* (Rainwater *et al.*, 1959). The study aimed to investigate empirically what advertisers hitherto had taken for granted: the cultural universe of their main advertising object: the Middle Majority Housewife. Rainwater and his colleagues combined demographic data similar to that of the old ABCD categories (they called it 'Index of Urban Status') with Thematic Appreciation Tests borrowed from consumer psychology and in-depth interviews borrowed from motivation research. The study generated an in-depth descriptive picture of the everyday life of the Housewives, including information on their psychological attitudes and relations to consumer goods. Early studies like this produced detailed pictures of consumer cultures that were still coupled to a particular class position. During the 1960s however, the variables used by Rainwater and his colleagues were developed into what became known as 'psychographic' variables usually encompassing the fields of 'Attitudes, Opinions and Interests' (Wells and Tigert, 1971; Demby, 1974). At the same time, advances in computer technology made it possible to employ a wide range of variables – 300 was not uncommon – and then use factor analysis to produce a number of variable clusters, to be represented theoretically as 'life styles' (Seth, 1970; Digg, 1966). The Methodological procedure was thus very different from what had been the case in the ABCD system. There, consumers had been segmented according to one variable (or one series of variables) denoting class position. Now, segments were no longer defined a priori, but rather deduced from the rich data material generated by extensive questioners. This meant that the overall picture that was generated was no longer a priori determined by class. Also, the number of variables relating directly to consumption, such as product, brand or media choice, tended to increase during the 1970s as the life-style survey became standard marketing practice through the impact of successful services such as Daniel Yankelovich's 'Yankelovich Monitor', founded in 1971, and later Arnold Mitchell and Stanford Research Institute's VALS, which began officially in 1978.

The inductive approach of psychographics meant that consumers were no longer depicted as structured according to some over-riding principle. It also meant that the particular segments generated could change over time. As William D. Wells recognized in his foreword to the American Marketing Association's 1974 volume on 'Lifestyle and Psychographics', this dynamic approach had developed as a response to a social environment that was perceived to be increasingly dynamic and marked by 'rapidly changing values' (Wells, 1974: v; cf. Rathnell, 1964). To put it in the words of an advertising professional writing in the middle of the decade (Ruth Ziff, head of Benton & Bowles' research department):

> We are living in an era of pluralism, non-conformity and rapid change. Racial groups are seeking a new identity and proposing separation rather than assimilation. Social mores have changed rapidly. The women's movement is positing changes that may affect our basic family structure. Styles of living and dress are indeed varied. Consumerism has become a major force. These changes make more hazardous than ever reliance on our own pre-conceptions or on data on the consumer that is scanty or outmoded. This then is another reason for turning to psychographics.
>
> (Ziff, 1974: 139)

Towards the branding paradigm

The availability of new and richer forms of information on consumers now coincided with the emphasis, introduced by motivation research, on the specific relations that could prevail between particular products and particular groups of consumers. In the 1960s, these factors combined to promote the emergence of 'life-style advertising', a precursor to contemporary branding. Life-style advertising was about making the product anticipate a certain attitude, mode or feeling. It was essential that this immaterial characteristic of the product be perceived as one of its innate qualities, and thus enact the extended qualities that were particular to the product. A 1969 Coca-Cola memorandum (from *The Pause that Refreshes* campaign) makes this point clearly:

Consumers see every ad or commercial for Coke as an extension of the product itself. Time and again in research studies people will comment, 'that's not Coca-Cola' when the ambience of the commercial or ad is not 'quality' or 'tasteful' or misses the way people see the product and how it fits the pulse of their daily lives. So it follows that a commercial for Coca-Cola should have the properties of the product itself. It should be a pleasurable experience, refreshing to watch and pleasant to listen to. It should reflect quality by being quality. And it should make you say, 'I wish I'd been there. I wish I had been drinking Coke with those people'.

(as cited in Rutherford, 1994: 57)

This philosophy was evident in so-called 'life-style' television advertising during the 1960s. Leo Burnett's 'Marlboro Man' commercial from 1963 (following the repositioning of Marlboro from a woman's cigarette to a 'filter cigarette for real men') broke rather radically with traditional tobacco advertising. Previously it had been common to socialize the cigarette in realistic representations of everyday life. Instead Marlboro chose to convey the product's connotations of macho ruggedness by connecting it to the theme of the Wild West and its cowboys, known almost exclusively through television. As copy-writer Jack Landy commented, the purpose was to accommodate 'youth [who] were reaching out for something or someone they could identify with' (Rutherford, 1994: 42). Similarly Coca-Cola and Pepsi-Cola produced a number of films where the purpose was to connect the product to an idea, experience or emotion to the product, often drawing on the imagery of the youth culture. Examples are Coca-Cola's 1969 'Hilltop' commercial featuring young people of 30 nationalities singing of altruism and world peace on a Hilltop in Italy ('I want to buy the world a Coke') or Pepsi's 'Pepsi Generation' from 1963 in which the product is projected as an intrinsic component of a new generational consciousness (Hollander, 1992).

In life-style advertising the product already featured an anticipation of a particular form of life, which is not connected to other products by means of code. Rather it emerges as a more or less free-floating sign to be assembled into the expression of a (more or less) sovereign consumer. This format was to remain highly influential during the 1970s and 1980s. But in the 1980s the life-style format began to be experienced as problematic. The first and most important problem was its almost exclusive reliance on advertising. In a highly diversified media environment, following the explosion of satellite and cable television and the availability of VCRs and remote controls, advertising had even less of an impact than before. Self-consciously 'post-modern advertising' like the Nike 'Revolution' commercial created by the Wieden+Kennedy agency, responded to this by going back to Bernbach *et al.*'s creative revolution and creating ads that toyed around with the intertext of (mainly) television culture (Berger, 2001). Similarly, the new possibilities for synergies and cross marketing provided by the emerging internet environment were actively utilized to multiply the channels available to marketing. Marketing thus took an increasingly multidimensional turn in the 1990s (see next chapter). Second, the kinds of data mining techniques that became available during the 1980s, together with the expansion of qualitative research produced a possibility of programming deeper and tighter relations between consumers and goods (or, increasingly, brands). Rather than just style or image, a particular brand could now be made to anticipate things like 'emotion', 'community' or 'reassurance' (Sherrington, 1995: 514). Of course, the idea that marketing should operate with other parameters beyond advertising had always been there, and it had been emphasized already in 1964 in Neil Borden's idea of the 'marketing mix' (involving, eventually the 4Ps – Product, Place, Price, Position – (in)famous to every beginning business school student). In the early 1980s, however, the new philosophy of Customer Relations Management, or CRM, radicalized this proposal. CRM built on the idea that it was more profitable to tie existing customers to the brand and build up brand loyalty, than to mass advertise for new ones. The idea was not entirely new, but now new market research techniques that combined data from a multitude of sources, like credit card records, bar code scans, media consumption surveys and demographics became available (Turow, 1997; Weiss, 1989). These allowed a much more detailed targeting of potential customers (building on 'mined' data profiles). Deploying this information, airlines, supermarkets and car-makers launched loyalty clubs, where customers would receive additional benefits in exchange for personal information. Soon these were supplanted with in-house magazines and the availability of information or services through call centres. As the importance of organizational symbolism and corporate branding grew simultaneously within management (see Chapter 5), it was not a big step to transforming these clubs into 'communities' kept together by a common 'identity'. This involved a radical step, however. No longer uniquely on the receiving end of information, offers or 'content' distributed through loyalty clubs, people were now constituted as active producers of community. People's 'natural' tendency to use consumer goods to produce social relations was consciously put to work.

Third, the new kind of information available permitted a tracking of the mobility of consumer practices and innovations. This enabled brand management to become more dynamic and open ended, moving with the productivity of consumer practice. This new mobility was institutionalized through the emergence of a new professional figure within the advertising industry, the account planner. The account planner was to work as third party to the creative team. His (or her) role was to guarantee a constant contact with the consumer (to 'speak for' the consumer) by means of (mostly) qualitative research. The account planner thus guaranteed a dynamic contact with actual consumer practices that had grown too mobile and transitory to be captured by any conventional 'Reality'. The figure of the account planner first emerged at the London agencies Boase, Massimi & Pollitt and JWT in the 1960s (Pollitt, 1979), but it was to have its real breakthrough in the late 1980s, when it was adopted by most large American (and subsequently global) advertising agencies (D'Souza, 1986; Frank, 1999). This in turn was connected to the emergence of brand management as the prevailing paradigm of advertising and marketing practice.

Conclusion

Marketing and advertising constructs a Reality (or 'real virtuality'), by means of which the 'truth, beauty and utility' that make up the value of goods can be organized. This Reality is in turn constructed on the basis of available information about consumers; it is erected on an informational interface. This chapter has shown how, during the twentieth century, this Reality of advertising has changed from representing a stable common consumption norm, attainable to different degrees by different consumers according to their allocation along a common ABCD typology, to representing the context of consumer practice as a set of evolving, mutually independent qualities tied first to life-styles and then to brands. The Reality of consumption has gone from a coherent monotheism – where all goods were the servants of the same rational middle class God – to paganism. This shift has been the consequence of the transformation of the informational interface available to marketing. After the impact of motivation research, market research changed from the simple 'nose counting' of individuals, whose situation within a particular predetermined category made their needs and preferences known, to the gathering of a large variety of variables linked not so much to particular individuals as to particular meanings or practices – purchasing patterns, values, media consumption, and so on. These were subsequently re-elaborated into particular life-styles. These new techniques permitted the decomposition of individual consumers into 'data-clouds' and their recomposition into representations of the context of consumption. Like contemporary forms of informational surveillance, they shifted the attention from the individual to the achievements of the social, 'the productive multitude' (Terranova, 2004: 122). This way the cultural context of consumption could be programmed, worked upon and come to function as a mechanism for the abstraction of value, as a form of immaterial capital.

The previous chapter described one of the pre-conditions for this, the emergence of a new consumer productivity spurred by electronic media. This chapter has shown how marketing has reacted to that development through the erection of a new informational interface able to capture that productivity. Contemporary branding is the outcome of this capitalist reaction towards the mass intellectuality made possible by electronic media, a reaction in itself made possible by such media and the new kinds of information processing capacities that they brought about. Next chapter will show how these two aspects come together in the brand.

4   Brand management

Brands have a history that goes back to long before the development of modern marketing. Historians often point to Josiah Wedgwood and his successful creation of the Wedgwood & Bentley brand of luxury china in industrializing eighteenth-century Britain (cf. Brewer and Porter eds, 1993; Wernick, 1991). In many ways, Wedgwood & Bentley anticipated the approach of contemporary brand management. Their catalogues and showrooms were designed to convey a particular 'shopping experience', as we would say today. In targeting the expanding middle class market they launched a line of less expensive china, that they gave the romantically suggestive name 'Etruria' (along with the factory that made it). Above all, they understood how to make public communication work for them. Recognizing how an expanding consumer society, and the concomitant rise of a new kind of immaterial 'pleasures of the imagination' (Brewer, 1997) was in the process of destabilizing the cultural boundaries between the classes, and how, consequently, the growing middle classes now sought to emulate the consumption habits of the aristocracy and the upper class, Wedgwood & Bentley invested in creating a high status image around their product. They achieved this by aggressively marketing a more exclusive line of hand-made china to aristocratic customers (often selling it below costs), by securing royal commissions, and by taking on expensive and often unprofitable special orders from aristocratic families. Once such an order had been completed, Wedgwood (who was the marketing genius) wasted no time in advertising the deed in London newspapers, directed at a middle class public. While they might have lost money on the individual vase or piece of pottery, they stood to gain much more from the publicity that such an aristocratic commission could procure: 'The Great People have had their Vases in their Palaces long enough for them to be seen and admired by the Middling Class of People, which Class we know are vastly, I had almost said, infinitely superior in number to the Great'.[1] Recognizing that the aristocracy worked as 'legislators in taste' Wedgwood prepared the company's entry on the German market by sending unsolicited packages of china to the German nobility and aristocracy. In short, Wedgwood *put the aristocracy to work* in producing a certain quality to be attached to the product, by giving it a place in the shared meanings and social relations that formed their now more visible lifeworld. Wedgwood was conscious of the fact that this socially constructed 'aura' might be as valuable as the material qualities of the product:

> How much of this general use, & estimation [of our china across the world], is owing to the mode of its introduction & how much to its real utility and beauty? are questions in which we may be a good deal interested for the government of our future Conduct. For instance, if a Royal, or Noble Introduction be necessary to the sale of an Article of Luxury, as real Elegance & beauty, then the Manufacturer, if he consults his own interest will bestow as much pains, & expense too if necessary, in gaining the former of these advantages, as he would in bestowing the latter.[2]

Thanks to their brand-image, Wedgwood & Bentley could extract a premium price of 8 pence for a dinner plate (the normal price for other Staffordshire potters in the 1770s was around 2 pence). At least in part, this difference was attributable to the work of public communication, skilfully managed by means of a 'Royal or Noble Introduction'.

The same basic principle stands at the heart of brand management today. Even though the techniques are far more sophisticated, and the environment far more complex and multifaceted, brand management is still essentially about putting public communication to work in ways that ether *add to* or *reproduce* the particular qualities that the brand embodies. It is these qualities that consumers subsequently pay for access to. They are the substance of the 'premium price' that consumers are prepared to pay for the branded good. Brand management is about putting public communication to work under managed forms, by providing a context where it can evolve in a particular direction. Indeed, this has become even more central as contemporary brand management often stresses the importance of moving beyond the conception of the brand as simply a 'maker's mark' or a sign of quality, to establish a relationship with consumers. Ideally, the brand should be conceived as a 'personality' with emotional or even ethical dimensions (Gobe, 2001). This also means positing consumers as active partners to a relationship and making what they do with or say about the brand matter to the evolution of its personality. The easiest way to do this is to quite simply appropriate the *common* that people spontaneously produce in their use of branded consumer goods.

Innovation

From the point of view of brand management, consumers use brands as means of production. Brand management, most rather emphatically stress, differs from 'modern' or Fordist marketing. It is not about imposing ways of using goods, or behaving or thinking as a consumer. Rather, it is about proposing branded goods as tools, or building blocks whereby consumers can create their own meanings. What people pay for, the idea goes, is not so much the brand itself as what they can produce with it: what they can *become* with it. To quote one successful American pop-management book: 'The power of any brand is simply how your associations with it make you feel' (Travis, 2000: 10). Customers are thus expected to add more or less personal dimensions to the brand, to accommodate it in their life-world, to produce something – a feeling, a personal relation, an experience – with it. The simplest way to make consumers work *for* the brand is then to simply appropriate the surplus that they produce in their normal use of branded goods.

One way that has been very popular in recent years is 'viral', 'guerrilla' or 'stealth' marketing. This technique involves stimulating consumers to generate a 'word of mouth' that distributes or speaks of the product. It puts to work the established interaction and communication networks of everyday life, where it is presupposed that brands play an integral part. Techniques range from spreading the product among a select, but influential clique of consumers, and then hoping that they will distribute it, and by doing so, rub off a bit of their prestige; through paying people to loudly order one's brand of drink in a bar, and other kinds of Real Life product placement (Godin, 2000). SMS messaging and email lend themselves very well to these kinds of marketing techniques. The viral marketing agency, 'The Viral Factory', produces online content, like the *Trojan Games* website that advertises condoms of the same name, featuring material from fake Olympic Games with a 'laddish' sexual angle. The idea is that (laddish) people will distribute the link to their friends and that the brand will thus be deployed in the everyday production of social relations through gossip and idle talk. Hotmail is a famous success story of viral marketing. By adding a tag line on its emails, it managed to spend only $500,000 on advertising, compared with the

$20 million of its competitor Juno, and achieved far superior results as users themselves acted as a marketing channel for the service (Jurveson and Draper, 1998). The idea behind viral marketing is not only that everyday spontaneous communication can help distribute and advertise the brand. But also that inserting the brand in social relations, making it a kind of medium through which the 'purposeless sociality and idle talk' (that according to Heidegger served to reproduce and give substance to the social) can transpire, adds intrinsically to the qualities associated with the brand.

A similar, if more established technique involves inserting the brand in, and trying to tap into already existing social networks or communities. Nike has been successful at (and much criticized for) tapping into inner city communities. The sneaker is introduced into the social economy of the 'ghetto'. Like rap music, it thereby acquires connotations that make it exciting to suburban middle class kids (Goldman and Papson, 1996; Vanderbildt, 1998). French Cognac companies (under heavy competition from aggressive Scottish pure malts) have begun to do the same thing, buying product placements in rap-lyrics among other things – since 'Puff Daddy's' 2002 hit 'Pass the Courvoisier' confirmed the place of cognac in 'pimp' life-style. The Gap has had a similar strategy in relation to the gay community, as has Absolut Vodka (Chasin, 2000). In Britain, the energy drink Red Bull began to appear in clubs and dance music festivals before it was marketed or sold anywhere else. Tired clubbers were offered free Red Bull (with or without Stolichnaya vodka) and Red Bull publicity was everywhere, including the play station game Wipeout, available in chill-out rooms and particularly geared at the dance music generation with a soundtrack by the Manchester duo The Chemical Brothers (Grant, 1999: 60, ff.). Red Bull thus became part of the dance music scene and could be marketed as such.

Through these techniques brands are inserted into existing networks of interaction and communication, and these are constituted as a means of distributing or adding dimensions of use-value to the brand, adding on things that one can perform with it. If the brand is established as part of a particular subcultural universe, it becomes possible to act as if one was part of, or better to act *in the style* of that universe, by using goods marked with the brand in question. By drinking Courvoisier, one can party in pimp style and Absolut vodka can be consumed in the style of the trend-setting inner city gay community (regardless of one's sexuality). Style, Dick Hebdige (1979) famously suggested, is what the subculture produces (often in an act of defiance): it is the most important form of its ethical surplus. It is also what brand management mainly appropriates.

The appropriation of style and its transformation into brand image is thus one of the simplest examples on how brand management exploits the productivity of consumers.

Consumers are also used as active partners to the product development process, as a kind of co-producers. In certain sectors, like the highly competitive American sneaker market, subjecting new models to consumer feedback before launching them on the market has become normal business practice. Nike and Reebok continuously subject new prototypes to 'kid's' judgement as to whether these are 'cool' or not, thus generating direct feedback into the product development process (Lee and Gordon, 2002). In general, product designers have come to rely much more on end-user feedback or even participation. One way of achieving this is to hire the kinds of people one plans to sell to. Fashion companies have done this for a long time. Diesel and Tommy Hilfiger both employ people that are representative of their target audience, encourage them to read, travel, go out and otherwise immerse themselves in their peer culture as much as possible, and then make use of their insights in developing new styles and fashions. Similarly, branded super-stores and fashion emporiums employ people whose personal character-istics fit with the brand (Pettinger, 2004). Benetton has a magazine, *Colors*, produced by young people that represent an ideal sample of the Benetton target group (Grant, 1999: 28; Gladwell, 1997; Seabrook, 2002). Similarly, 'trendiness' is an important factor for luxury brand companies when recruiting (adult) personnel (Stalnaker, 2002). Alterna-tively, one can observe and study the target group. Not unexpectedly, the 'branding revolution' has been accompanied by a boom in the qualitative market research industry (Feldwick, 1999; Gordon, 1999; Upshaw, 1995). While qualitative research has been around for a long time, recent approaches are not so much interested in the psychological as in the cultural and sociological aspects of consumer practice. What one tries to capture is not so much individual taste and motivation as the social meanings collectively produced in the interaction between consumers. Consequently, the well-established focus group is being supplanted by a rising popularity of ethnographic methods. Companies like Motorola, Microsoft, McDonald's and MTV regularly employ ethnographic studies to keep up with their target audiences. MTV conducts regular field trips where, in Senior Vice President for Strategy, Todd Cunningham's words 'we get a great chance to go out and rifle through kids' closets and go through their music collection and go to nightclubs with them' (Cunningham, 2002). More recently, market researchers have come to employ consumers to do their own self-research. In order to find out about young people's attitudes to alcoholic drinks, the French drinks marketing firm Allied Domecq employed university students as researchers. Based on the principle that 'nobody can understand a community better than that community itself' they were charged with researching their own peer culture. The idea was that this would give a better rendering not only of the reasons for drinking but of the general cultural and social *context* in which drinking took place: 'We wanted to explore their personal values, their feelings about their lives, their universe, and their hopes and dreams. Essentially we wanted to think beyond current market conditions and business needs and to be curious about the future' (Pegram and Acreman, 2000). Similarly in order to perform a general survey of European youth culture, the British marketing company Futurebrand simply put a group of young adults on a bus, toured them around Europe and charged them with the task to socialize with their peers and see what was going on (Carter, 2002). This research, like most recent ethnographic market research is guided by the ambition to map and eventually appropriate the meanings that brands and products acquire as part of the life process of consumers.

Trend spotting, or 'cool hunting' firms have driven this one step further. These firms have developed during the last ten years or so. They provide a number of services that are based on a continuous surveillance of the social. Their focus is mainly, but not exclusively on the youth market (considered the vanguard of the consumer market as a whole). Youth Intelligence is a New York-based company that focuses on 8–35 year olds (the so called Generations X and Y). They provide a variety of services for their clients: information on Macro (general) and Micro (market or product specific) trends; a 'brand tracker' that evaluates the standing of brands 'with respect to consumer awareness and "cool factor"', examples of trend products and life-style investigations. They also perform market research on particular brands and services, and offer their services as consultants in product development, brand renewal, PR or corporate brainstorming sessions. Among their wide range of clients are media companies like Fox (television), Artisan Entertainment (film) and Electronic Arts (computer games), cosmetics and fashion companies (L'Oreal and Polo Jeans), publishers (Cosmopolitan), communications (Motorola, Sony, Virgin Mobile), advertising agencies (Ogilvy & Mather) and big brand companies like Nike, McDonald's and Procter & Gamble. Other leading companies like Look-look and Teen Research have similarly impressive lists of clients. While Youth Intelligence uses traditional forms of market research like focus groups and ethnographies (often set in 'young people's own worlds' like 'skate parks, teahouses, pizza parlours, or even their homes'), the main source of the information they provide is a network of '300 trendsetters across 3 age groups: 14–18, 19–24, 25–30'. Similarly, the Zandl group recruits '3000 people between the ages of 8–24 to find out what is or isn't cool'.

What distinguishes the young people employed by these agencies is that they make up a group of expert consumers. They are the people who impersonate a trend before it materializes, Says Claire Brooks, executive strategic planning director at the Lambesis Agency:

> There are a lot of early mainstream people who really think that they are trendsetters – the people who say 'I really love Gap' and you just think 'Yeah, you really don't know about that do you?' Whereas the true trendsetter will be making her own clothing. Or her friend will have started a boutique or a fashion line or whatever.
>
> (Grossman, 2003)

Unlike the aristocracy that Wedgwood approached, the people approached by trend scouts have a particular expertise in the field of consumption that need not be connected to a more general elite status, or even to high standing or competence in other fields. Indeed, as Alicia Quart remarks in her report on American high-school girls employed by trend-scouting companies, these are generally not people who enjoy the highest status in other fields. Rather it is a matter of the 'slightly awkward or overweight or not conventionally pretty'. She speculates that '[W]hile many teenagers are branded, the ones most obsessed with brand names feel they have a lack that only superbranding will cover over and insure against social ruin' (Quart, 2003: 31). Be this as it may, trend scouts are interested in the people who possess an expertise in predicting and or even anticipating fads and fashions, who have a motivation to constantly stay at the top of the field, to use Bourdieu's terminology. These may be extraordinary creative and gifted individuals, but as Bourdieu argues (in the case of artistic production) their edge consists mainly in their ability (and motivation) to interpret the position of others. Trendsetters are what they are because they are the first to articulate and materialize what everybody subsequently recognizes as general knowledge. They thus provide a way of appropriating the socialized productivity of the particular field in its entirety.

But what is it they produce? What is 'coolness'? The significance of the term *cool*, probably goes back to the Yoruba concept of *Itutu*. It has been preserved in the culture of American plantation slaves where it has come to signify a certain challenge or defiance. Indeed, Poutain and Robins (2000) in tracing the genealogy of cool include such antecedents as the British aristocratic reserve, and the *spezzatura* of Italian courtiers, as well as the anti-establishment attitude of the twentieth-century *avant-garde* and counter-culture. They conclude that *cool* should be translated as a kind of achieved defiance. It is an attitude of opposition that one produces and assembles in front of a challenge. They go on to define the meaning of 'cool' as a mass-phenomena of consumer society:

> [W]e see cool as a permanent state of private rebellion. Permanent because cool is not just some 'phase that you go through' something that you 'grow out of', but rather something that once attained remains for life; private because Cool is not a collective political response, but a stance of individual defiance.
>
> (Poutain and Robins, 2000: 18)

In this sense, coolness refers to the capacity on the part of consumers in their collective production of meaning, in their mass intellectuality, to produce private and apolitical forms of resistance or evasion in relation to the power of marketing and other institutions of consumer culture. As in the case of the appropriation of style, capturing cool is a matter of incorporating and profiting from the resistance that consumers spontaneously produce. (Indeed, the antithesis of cool is understood to be 'commodification': One ceases to be cool at the moment in which one's style becomes appropriated as part of the mainstream. Conversely, continued coolness builds on a continuous capacity for stylistic resistance.) Cool hunting is one of the institutional mechanisms by means of which 'consumer resistance' becomes 'a form of market-sanctioned cultural experimentation through which the market rejuvenates itself' (Holt, 2002: 90).

If in the times of Simmel and Veblen, innovation in consumer tastes and trends were the business of the bourgeoisie and their children, today it is the business of the consumer proletariat in its natural state of alienation and defiance. It is the fact that some consumers *do not identify* with the prevailing norms of consumer culture that makes their agency valuable as creative labour power.

Reproduction

All consumers cannot be innovative and not everybody can be cool. Few people have the time and energy to invest in a continuous production of resistance, 'authenticity' or originality. But, from the point of view of brand management, all consumers use goods to produce a significant share of the solidarities and shared meanings that anchor them in their life-world. Consequently, an important task for brand management is to ensure that the ongoing production of a common social world on the part of consumers proceeds in ways that reproduce a distinctive *brand image*, and that strengthens the *brand equity* – the productive potential that the brand has in the minds of consumers – which is understood as the most important factor behind brand value.

To ensure this, brand management uses what Michel Foucault (1991) once called government. This is different from discipline, his other main concept of modern power. One does not so much give orders or shape actions according to a given norm, as much as one works from below, by providing an ambience in which freedom is likely to evolve in particular ways. One works with and through the freedom of the subject (Dean, 1999; Rose, 1999). Government is about the political constitution of life forms. In brand management this is achieved through the provision of particular ambiences that frame and partially anticipate the agency of consumers. As Lury (2004) argues, the brand works as a kind of 'platform for action' that is inserted into the social and works to 'program' the freedom of consumers to evolve in particular directions. While it is not impossible for consumers to break with the expectations inscribed in these ambiences – as the pranks performed by groups like Ad-Busters, or the aloof coolness of elite consumers show – the task of brand management is to create a number of resistances that make it difficult or unlikely for consumers to experience their freedom, or indeed their goals, in ways different from those prescribed by the particular ambience. At the most abstract level, the construction of such ambiences proceeds through the management of media culture.

The development of brand management during the 1990s was paralleled by a profound transformation of the media landscape. New technologies and the new regulatory environment put in motion a significant structural transformation of the media and culture industries. During the 1990s the American media and communications industry saw a number of mergers and acquisitions that resulted in the field being dominated by a few global giants like AOL-Time-Warner, Disney and Viacom. Their growth and diversification was truly astonishing. In 1988 Disney was a $2.8 billion per year amusement park and cartoon company; in 1998 Disney had $25 billion in sales divided between television and radio (ABC, Buena Vista Productions), internet (InfoSeek), film studios (Miramax, Touchstone), a cruise line, a residential community

(Celebration), sport teams and 660 Disney retail stores around the world. Viacom, a '$600 million syndication and cable outfit' in 1988, did $14.5 billion worth of business in 1998 and MTV, its perhaps most important asset reached 300 million homes, or one quarter of the world's television households (McChesney, 1999: 19, 94, 108). In part these mergers were driven by the economies of scale of the media business, in part they were a reaction to the new diversity of that environment made possible by new technologies like cable, satellite, VCR and the internet. But these transformations were also driven by an increasing recognition that the key to future profits lay in marketing strategies that could reach across different media platforms (Schiller, 1999). Extended across different media platforms, particular brands of content, like *Star Wars* or *Lord of the Rings* could be present in a plurality of circumstances (films, toys, fast food, games, candy, and so on) and thus accumulate commercially valuable attention from a whole diversity of consumer practices. Indeed, the transformation of the media environment in the 1990s both tended to diminish the effectiveness of advertising and – through the integration of media culture into life in general and the proliferation of new informational tools – enable a more far-reaching subsumption of the productivity of consumers.

The emerging strategy consisted in marketing what Marshall (2002) has called 'intertextual commodities'. When a particular media product (or 'content') can be promoted across different media channels and sold in different formats, what is marketed is not so much films or books, as 'content brands' that can travel between and provide a context for the consumption of a number of goods or media products. Thus brands like *The Lion King, Harry Potter*, the *X-Files* and *Britney Spears* come as music, film, books, games, McDonald's hamburgers, cosmetics, clothing and websites – to mention just a few possibilities. Computer games are a popular form of such extensions. In 2001, licensed games (like Toy Story or Harry Potter) accounted for 45 of the 100 top UK games. Similarly, some successful games have generated (generally less successful) films, like *Wing Commander, Tomb Raider* and *Final Fantasy* (Kerr and Flynn, 2003: 103–4). Indeed, Nintendo was one of the first brands to systematically employ such cross-marketing. Starting in the late 1980s, *SuperMario Bros* came as T-shirts, watches, breakfast cereal, sleeping bags, dolls, magazines, wallpaper, snacks and a number of similar objects. The links between these objects created an ambience within which kids were free to produce the particular 'finishing touch' that adapted the product to their life-world – by using the objects provided or enacting some of the narrative content of the ambience, in play for example. These allowed (mostly adolescent) consumers to live in a *Nintendo* universe which transpired different kinds of media and activities (Provenzo, 1991: 15, ff.). What *Nintendo* sold was in effect a branded environment that provided a particular context for 'kids' consumer agency; where it was likely to evolve in a particular direction, towards the reproduction of a particular brand image. With its historical origins in 'kid culture', where connections between toys, media culture, fast food and candy developed at an early stage, the form of the 'intertextual commodity' serves to give a commercial space that includes a number of diverse and not entirely anticipated activities. The intertextual commodity, in effect provides an ambience where a form of patterned play' (Marshall, 2002: 72), a creative or even playful agency can evolve on the premises of the brand.

In a diversified media environment a coherent and well-managed ambience fulfils two important functions. First, it provides a context for consumer action within which a particular consumer good or media product can acquire additional dimensions of use-value. In modernity, such contexts were either provided 'naturally' through class traditions or other forms of 'rooted' communities, or by means of the 'ideological state apparatus' and the code of value that it helped implementing (particularly through its mediatic branch: public service television). As such forms of community wither away, the brand replaces them as a commercially managed context of action, where, as in the case of the MTV community, a certain attitude, a certain modality of consumption is anticipated. Second, such ambiences serve to capture the attention of consumers who habitually move between media platforms. Previously, such attention could be captured by a particular physically situated media technology, such as, paradigmatically, the television set in the living room. But with the hyper-mediation of the life-world and with the emergence of technologies like remote controls, VCRs and TiVos that allow a personalization of media consumption, consumers are less subject to the technological power of particular media platforms.

The same thing goes for advertising. It is generally recognized that the new media environment, new 'interactive' technologies, and a heightened media literacy on the part of consumers, make them less likely to accept traditional 'hard sell' advertising messages. The response on the part of advertising has been both a greater recourse to reflexivity and irony and, most importantly, a shift over from advertising to brand management. While selling messages are still prominent, a growing importance is attached to the ability to create the brand as a mediatic ambience. The main strategy here is to place the product in different mediatic (and Real Life) circumstances. Hollywood blockbusters (in particular the Bond films, in themselves a sort of consumerist manifesto) have pioneered this tendency, and television serials like *Sex and the City* or the British *Coronation Street* now generate significant revenues from fees paid by advertisers to make sure that the computer is a Macintosh, the car a Saab and the cell phone a Motorola. (Sometimes, as in the 2000 adventure drama, *Cast Away*, the placed brand, in this case FedEx, becomes a central character in the narrative; Rodgers, 2002.) Indeed, much of the logic of the media industries is oriented to the search for (or invention of) content brands like *The Spice Girls* or *Britney Spears* that can easily be extended across different media platforms and used for product tie-ins and cross-promotions. The purpose of such strategies is to create a network of intertextual links that suggests a coherent modality of use or enjoyment for the product.

With the 'mediatization of consumption' (Janson, 2002) the distinction between material product and promotional message tends to be less clear. This also means that material goods themselves can become a channel for the construction of a branded ambience. Since out-sourcing and information technologies have contributed to de-skill the production of material objects, a number of brand centred companies have embarked on a wave of brand extensions, adding new product lines to their brands. Nike began selling sports shoes, now the company sells a wide range of shoes, athletic fashion, accessories, and eventually there will also be a Nike television channel. Starbuck's sells coffee, as well as other snacks, clothes and accessories, and have tried (unsuccessfully) to enter the books and records market. Of course, one purpose of such brand extensions is to capture additional customers. Someone who cannot afford a Mercedes car, might afford and want a Mercedes bike or watch. In this sense they do the work that cross-media synergies do for media companies. But these products also become a kind of medium in themselves. They embody and carry the brand identity into new and diverse fields. In the end, the brand identity is embodied in the many linkages created by different products and different media and real life placements. For example, BMW has worked hard over the last ten years to establish a particular BMW quality that transpires its products and its organization. They have done this by advertising and marketing their cars and motorcycles in traditional ways, by placing them in various mediatic and real life contexts, by sponsoring exhibitions and events, and producing action films that evolve around the brand, available on the internet for download. BMW has also built an 'event and delivery centre' outside Munich, a kind of brand palace (or 'brandscape'; cf. Riewolt,

2002) where advanced architecture and design embodies the BMW experience. BMW has also engaged in brand extensions. Apart from cars, BMW sells toys, bikes, clothes, pens, calendars and other accessories. These objects all contribute to establishing the particular quality of the BMW brand. Through establishing and managing links between these objects, and different placements of the brand, BMW creates an inter-textual space that spans across media culture into real life – in which the essence of the brand, the quality of experience that it stands for can become manifest. The brand experience is realized by BMW consumers who can derive a way of relating to their cars and by non-owners who derive ways of relating to their not owning a car. Such guided 'envy' similarly contributes to building up the standing of the brand, and supposedly enhancing the experience of owners. While many of these brand-centred companies sell relatively expensive, luxury 'experiences' – like Tiffany's, Gucci, Prada or Luis Vuitton – not all do. More affordable examples of the same logic are Benetton, Swatch and Heineken. What they have in common is that a substantial part of the value of what they sell, in some cases the greatest part, derives not from particular material commodities, but from the context of consumption that they create through intertextual linkages formed between different commodities and the brand's different presences in media culture and in real life. The branded context works as a tool that makes it possible to create a particular meaning, relation or experience.

The use of advertising, product placements and brand extensions moves at the most abstract level. Here the power of brand management is limited to promoting a particular mood or feeling, and to policing the image of the brand, making sure that undesirable modalities of use do not receive publicity, as in the frequent censorship of movies and other media texts on the part of commercial sponsors (Wasko, 1994). Other tech-niques aim at a deeper intervention in the ways in which consumers actually do use or think about products.

One medium that has acquired a certain popularity is physical space. Recently there has been a proliferation of themed commercial environ-ments, restaurants like Starbucks or Café Nero in the UK, and TGI Friday's; retail environments like Barnes & Noble, mega-stores like the Tommy Hilfiger superstore in Los Angeles, Niketowns and Virgin Mega-stores just about anywhere (Ritzer, 1999). One key strategy of retailing in general has been to introduce the entertainment or 'e-factor' into everything; to transform the anonymous 'non-places' where modern (or 'supermodern'; Augé, 1998) shopping took place into the kinds of places that 'involve a concentration of our intentions, our attitudes, purposes and experiences' (Sherry, 1998: 6). Of course, the e-factor as such is not new. The history of consumer culture has shown how the provision of spectacle has been a crucial element, from the arcades and department stores of the late nineteenth century and on (Benjamin, 1983; Bowlby, 1985). George Ritzer (1999) draws a continuity between turn-of-the-century commercial spectacle and the simulated environments that serve to 're-enchant' today's consumer experience. He also hints at an important difference. Older forms of commercial spectacle were produced to be consumed passively, or at least in a kind of awe-struck silence. Consumers were to be overcome by the beauty of it all, to let themselves by guided around by salespersons, to let the environment take control of them. As Rachel Bowlby has shown, the early development of supermarkets coincided with the growth of elaborate control strategies aiming to produce a situation where 'the initiative is with the shelves, rather than with the shopper' (Bowlby, 2000: 32). Contemporary themed environments on the other hand aim not so much at passive admiration as at involvement. The distinction between the shopping mall and the amusement park is withering away, Ritzer claims (1999: 134). Consumers are invited to actively co-perform the themed experience. As Ritzer points out, this experience generally results from social interaction among consumers, as much as from the features of the physical environment (Ritzer, 1999: 90). Niketown in Chicago for example, is built on the principle of the constant activity of consumers. They are invited to try on shoes, test athletic gear, to use the indoor basketball court as a space for 'mystical participation in the world of Michael Jordan' (Sherry, 1998: 126). The role of salespersons is minimal (Peñaloza, 1999). Rather, the store is built on the principle of the theme park: it provides series of attractions around which consumers are encouraged to interact. This interaction frequently takes place across generations, as the store is full of parents who bring their children. Consumers are thus not just awed by the Michael Jordan statue, but that awe is enacted collectively as parents and children interact. Together they perform an event where the truth of the Nike values – that you can 'Just Do It' – acquires a significance that goes far beyond the accomplishments of a particular athlete. It becomes part of that shared experience, that meaningful 'quality time' spent with your children that Americans cherish so much. In fact, the primary purpose of the store is not to sell Nike products (as this would give other retailers unfair competition), but rather to provide a space where consumers can interact to perform an experience of the brand as somehow important to, or even part of their ordinary lives, where they are made to live the brand. As Sherry argues: 'Nike's brand essence is both embodied in the built environment and realized in apprehension, in an act of co-creation' (1998: 138). The Nike superstore, Lisa Peñaloza (1999) suggests, is a place where consumers produce meaning around the brand by performing a place of it in their own life histories. The themed environment provides an ambience for the productive interaction between consumers. It aims to ensure that the shared meaning or the social relation that they create more or less conforms to the parameters of the brand image. There are many other examples of such themed environments. At Ralph Lauren you are meant to behave as if you were in an English Gentlemen's club. Tommy Hilfiger, Emporio Armani and Diesel all use lights, design, music and the demeanour of personnel to encourage consumers to co-perform a particular ambience. The Prada commercial space in New York is famous for its use of architecture to entice consumers to perform interpretative work around the brand, as is the Hermès space in Tokyo (Manovich, 2001). These are all upscale examples, but the principle of involving consumers extends to more ordinary places as well. At McDonald's, clowns, the heavily scripted roles of personnel, bright coloured uniforms and Disney toys with your Happy Meal encourage the performance of wholesome family fun (cf. Ritzer, 1999). At Starbucks, the smoke-free environment, the schooled Zen-like attitude of the 'baristas', blues music and books from Oprah Winfrey's own book club encourage the performance of a laid back attitude appropriate to a west coast urban intellectual of the low to middle-brow kind. In these spaces consumers are set free in a controlled environment to engage in an 'act of co-creation': they produce an identity or a common social world using the means of production and the hints provided by the themed environment.

Yet another widespread technique entails the creation of branded communities. This idea goes back to the 1980s and the simultaneous popularity of Customer Relations Management, and availability of detailed consumer profiles (mined from large data banks). Deploying this information, airlines, supermarkets and car-makers launched loyalty clubs, were customers would receive additional benefits in exchange for personal information. Soon these were supplanted with in-house magazines and the availability of information or services through call centres. As the importance of organizational symbolism and corporate branding grew simultaneously within management (see next section), it was not a big step to transforming these clubs into 'communities' kept together by a common 'identity'. This involved an additional step, however. No longer uniquely on the receiving end of information, offers or 'content' distributed through loyalty clubs, people were now constituted as active producers of community. People's 'natural' tendency to use consumer goods to produce social relations was consciously put at work. Supermarkets were pioneers in the first respect. British supermarkets like Tesco and Sainsbury's both created ties to their customers through membership cards, special discounts, direct mailing and company publications. They make ties *between* customers possible through social events like cooking courses, gourmet dinners and wine tasting. (This approach was first launched by Nestlé in the 1980s. The company organized Italian cooking clubs around its newly purchased pasta brand Buitoni; Joachimsthaler and Aaker, 1997.) Some brands like Jeep and Harley Davidson routinely organize 'brandfests' where users can come together, improve their skills at using the product and, most importantly, socialize and create community ties. Harley Davidson has been particularly successful in creating a feeling of community around the brand, defined by a particular 'biker ethos' where true biker status is contingent on participation in a branded Harley gathering. (Harley Davidson is also one of the few brands that users routinely tattoo on their bodies; McAlexander and Shouten, 1998; Wolf, 1999.) New media like the internet and computer games (often in combination) have proven apt to stimulate managed community interaction (see Chapter 5). Many companies have launched sites were customers are invited to interact not only with the company, but also among themselves. Lego, for example, has launched a sophisticated website around its 'Bionicle' sub-brand. The site has generated fervent traffic as users interact through games and message boards. Such interaction is also directly used by Lego marketers and designers to develop the brand (Brickner, 2003). Multi-user computer games are another way to stimulate social interaction, particularly when targeting younger 'Generation Y' consumers who are acquainted with the medium. Motorola recently launched an interactive game called PartyMoto where users were to use chat and SMS to acquire points from other users. These points would eventually give them the community status required to enter the PartyMoto virtual nightclub where they could assume a wide variety of characters as the interactivity proceeded on a new level. Companies like Pepsi, IBM, Ford and Siemens have also used interactive 'advergames' to generate consumer interaction around their brands (Rodgers, 2002).

Contemporary brand management presupposes that the value of brands does not primarily derive from the qualities of the products that wear their mark. It is something else. The brand resides at the 'social' and even 'spiritual' level (Gad, 2000: 147, ff.); it embraces the whole relationship between a product and its consumer (Cowley, 1999: 12). Building a brand empire is 'about staking out emotional turf in our consciousness' (Wolf, 1999: 226). 'A product is no more than an artefact around which customers have experiences – brands are the total sum of those experiences' (Bedbury and Fenichell, 2002: 16); the key to its value resides in the 'emotional links' that it can create with its audience. Brands provide a propertied micro-context of consumption, it suggests ways in which a product or service can be experienced, related to or 'felt'. While product placements, themed environments, sponsorship, event marketing and branded communities are important, there is also a recognition that this brand identity is only *realized* insofar as consumers are involved in its co-creation. It is only when consumers let brands be part of their lives, when brands initiate 'enduring relationships' with consumers or become 'living ideas that can transform people's lives' (Grant, 1999: 379) that brand identity – the context of action that the brand represents – becomes a real use-value that people are prepared to pay extra for. Brand managers do of course contribute to the construction of brand image – through smart marketing or media placements. But most of their work consists in managing the autonomous production process that consumers engage in: to make sure that the common social world that they produce by means of the brand (a new street style, an experience of family bonding at McDonald's, an experience of empowerment with Nike) adds to the brand by either innovating or reproducing its desired set of qualities. Brand management contains a variety of techniques that all aim at controlling, pre-structuring and monitoring what people do with brands, so that what these practices do adds to its value. It is about ensuring that the means of consumption effectively become means of production; that the ethical surplus that consumers produce also becomes a source of surplus value. What distinguishes contemporary brand management is then not simply that it posits a producerly attitude on the part of consumers, but also that it intervenes deeply into the context of everyday life to make that producerly attitude – the media-enhanced productivity of consumers – effectively generate value. The brand becomes a hyper-socialized, de-territorialized factory.

The corporate brand

To marketing, goods might fulfil a wide variety of needs and functions, but brands are primarily to be understood as resources for the construction of a self and its social moorings. The purpose of brand management is to transform brands into 'popular ideas that people live by' (Grant, 1999: xi); to create 'enduring relations' with customers (Gad,

2000); to make the brand into one of the many significant others that anchor people to reality: 'Just as people have friends and colleagues who play different roles in their lives, they have brands that serve the same purpose' (Pattersen, 1999: 410). It is supposed that people use brands to build solidarity, meaning, experiences – all the things that are supposedly no longer provided by the social context to the same extent, or in an equally straightforward manner as before. This idea of the brand as a response to the existential insecurity of 'late' or 'post' modern societies (Beck, 1992; Giddens, 1991; Bauman, 1992) developed within brand management during the 1990s as a reaction to the much hyped phenomenon of 'Generation X'. 'X'rs had grown up with the disintegration of modern communities and securities – from the nuclear family to their own future career paths – and the almost complete media saturation of everyday life. Consequently, they had no stable beliefs, no enduring commitments and no trust in established institutions. It was supposed that brands could come in and fill this void (Ritchie, 1995). Commenting on the observation that, among British Xrs, only 13 per cent claimed to 'trust politicians', while 85 per cent claimed that they trusted Marks & Spencer, one article suggested that '[a]s social structures are dismantled, why cannot brands such as Marks and Spencer, Boots and Mars replace them?' (Hatfield, 1993). Like older forms of community, sustained by tradition, class or local culture, brands provide a context in which objects can take on new dimensions of meaning; where they can be used to produce an ethical surplus that enables a person to become a subject. As a *capitalist* response to the post-modern condition of insecurity and reflexivity, however, brands also position this production of identity (or dimensions thereof) in ways that make it add to the immaterial capital of the brand, the brand equity that is the source of its value.

This subsumption of the production of identity as a form of immaterial labour is perhaps pushed furthest in the case of the corporate brand. The history of corporate branding goes back to the early years of the twentieth century. In the United States new large corporations like AT&T, General Electric and General Motors met with criticism from labour unions, attacks from muckraking journalists, and 'a widespread perception of the giant corporation as impersonal, aloof and devoid of any "human soul"' (Marchand, 1998: 131). As a response they invested in (and developed the techniques of) Public Relations, to convince that their purpose was not greed or raw hunger for profit, but that they were in fact guided by higher motives, endowed with a 'consciousness' or even a 'soul'. Just as today, the construction of such a 'corporate image' was not only aimed at convincing a critical public of the corporation's good intentions and humane values, but also aimed at creating internal coherence among its employees (this became increasingly crucial as the complexity of organizations grew), and at boosting its standing among shareholders and other interested parties. Consequently, advertising, 'aditorials' and other forms of favourable publicity were paralleled by efforts to strengthen the solidarity, commitment and 'well being' of employees. Companies such as General Motors or the National Cash Register Company employed social workers, threw dances and other social events, offered lectures on subjects of public interest and classes in sewing and cooking, medical care and callisthenics on the job, or as in the case of Heinz, compulsory, bi-weekly manicures (Marchand, 1998; Koehn, 2001: 43, ff.). Similarly, architecture and design was deployed to give a recognizable and coherent identity to the corporation. In the postwar years, the idea of the company as a 'corporate citizen' working for the common good and in touch with the public opinion of its consumers and employees would become a significant element of the American model spread in Europe by the Marshall Aid (Carew, 1987).

Until the 1970s, the work of creating a corporate image was largely the business of public relations agencies and design bureaux. And the purpose was to show how the corporation fitted into a given national community: how what was good for General Motors was also good for America; how AT&T respected the values of small town America; how General Electric kept families together and facilitated the labour of the housewife. However, in the 1970s, the tradition of corporate image work advanced by PR professionals and designers met with an interest in corporate identity on the part of management scholars and the emerging profession of management consultants. While still concerned about maintaining the feeling of the corporation as a 'community' and guaranteeing the solidarity of employees, their interests were slightly different. The development of the professional management consultant – and indeed the whole development of 'management' in its contemporary form, as a capitalist technique of governance that focuses on social relations, identity and culture – was part of an overall restructuring of post-war capitalism, a 'new capitalist spirit' to use Boltanski and Chiapello's (1999) term. Four important tendencies had been in motion since the mid-1960s. First, the rise of a new category of knowledge workers or 'symbol analysts' employed in the production of the immaterial content of commodities posed different demands on management. The kinds of labour that these people engaged in were less susceptible to fitting into Taylorist managerial techniques (Heelas, 2002; Reich, 1991). Second, information technology made work more abstract and heightened 'the need for positive motivation and internal commit-ment' (Zuboff, 1988: 291). Third, new rapid product innovation and the mobility of market segments, posed new demands of flexibility on the organization. It had to be able to re-create itself and in rapid adaptation to a mobile and transitory environment (Whetten and Godfrey, 1998). Fourth, the dissolution of an older work ethic, the Fordist working class, and the nuclear family made workers increasingly homeless. Together with the diminishing significance of national cultures, this raised the possibility that the corporation could work as their main source of identity and existential meaning (Hochschild, 1997). (Shell is not Dutch – it is its own ethical universe; Fomburn and Rindova, 2000.) The response to these tendencies was what became known as the corporate brand (Olins, 2000). While corporate branding shared many techniques with previous corporate image work, the purpose was different. The corporate image tradition had tried to inscribe the corporation within an existing, national community, to show how it embraced and nurtured certain generally shared values. Corporate branding, on the other hand, was about constituting the corporation as a specific community, endowed with its own particular values, no longer subjected to the values of nation or family. The corporate image tradition sought to spread the values of the corporation to its public and to its employees. The assump-tion was that these values somehow preceded or transcended those of its employees. In corporate branding, on the other hand, the aim is increasingly to make employees produce the identity of the organization, and at the same time produce themselves as members of the organization. In developing their new corporate guidelines, Shell engaged employees in seminars and workshops in order to ensure that the resulting values 'came from below' and were actually representative of what employees thought about the organization. An additional benefit of thus engaging employees in reflecting on the ethical dimensions of the corporation is that this gives them an opportunity to elaborate on their own relations to the corporation. At the same time as they produce the ethical values of the corporation they produce themselves as members of the corporation (Fomburn and Rindova, 2000). Indeed, an important aspect of corporate branding is to create an ambience that activates employees in particular ways, that puts their freedom to work in producing the social relations that make up the corporation and themselves as members of it. The American conglomerate KI Koch has famously implemented a corporate culture in which employees are set free to make their own decisions at every level, but are encouraged to do so according to a framework deeply influenced by microeconomic models. There are no budgets. The individuals, on the other hand are expected and trained to constantly think and make decisions that maximizes the value of the firm. Barney and Stewart (2000) tell how a secretary saw a newly hired manager making photocopies. She approached him and suggested that since 'the opportunity cost for me making the photocopies is 50, for you it is 175, I will make the copies. In the meantime you will figure out a way to add 175 in value to the firm'. Similarly, Maravelias (2003) observes how, in the case of the multinational financial services company Skandia, the high trust culture that the company prides itself of in order to ensure a flexible and adaptable organization was in fact based on the complete absence of any kind of stability or enduring frames. Individuals in the organization felt compelled to constantly *produce* trust, to make themselves trustworthy participants in the 'culture' by maximizing their involvement in the social relations that made up the organization. Indeed, to work towards such an inclusion in the 'culture of trust' was necessary to secure one's career advancement or even place in the company. As one product manager states: 'If you do not constantly take new initiatives, come up with new ideas, if you do not work long hours, etc. you would probably end up in a small corner somewhere.' Individuals took initiatives to new projects, worked overtime and teamed up with new people, not because they were given directives to do so, but because of the absence of directives and the general lack of trust in the environment. The culture of 'trust' became a way of making individuals put large shares of their subjectivity, their capacity to communicate, relate and form emotional bonds at the disposal of the company, without there being any explicit pressure on them to do this, nor any guidelines for how it should be done: 'No one forces you to do it, but you still feel that you have to'. This absence of rules also meant that there were no official limits for how far that involvement could go. Unlike the case of the classic bureaucracy, the necessity to constantly produce one's own trustworthy status had eliminated any distinction between the private and the official self. As Luhmann (1979) has observed, trust is contingent on the capacity to expose personal uniqueness. Here too, personal authenticity was the key to inclusion. A person who merely conformed to general norms would eventually become a calculable factor in specific situations, but he or she would not be someone trustworthy enough to become a general organizational resource, able to circulate freely in the fluid work environment. As an employee put it: 'In this fluid environment you don't trust someone who appears to hide his [sic] personal standpoints behind some stereotypical and impersonal role, you need to see who you are actually dealing with.' At the same time, there was a constant need to adapt the authentic self that one presented to the highly implicit and informal rules of the organization. As a product manager said: 'In this company we tend to promote people with a certain attitude, rather than those with particular skills.' Indeed, 'personality', was generally understood to be more important than formal competence.

It was thus up to employees, in their attempts to become trustworthy participants, to produce the linkages, the social relations and emotional ties that kept the organization together. At the same time, strategic management seemed to understand its role as a kind of GOD, or Generator Of Diversity. 'I think it would be incorrect to say that someone is actually controlling this organization. The core group is not in control, but they still play an important role by constantly trying to produce a feeling of restlessness in the organization, a feeling of "no haste no pause".' The company president shared this view: 'In terms of cause and effect, we have very limited control over the company's procedures.'

> I travel back and forth across the Atlantic and meet as many people as I can. During these meetings I tell them what other business units do and I ask questions about their plans, new ideas, etc, and try to twist and turn with their arguments in order to make them think a little bit differently about their operation. I never know exactly what will come out of these meetings. My objective is not to reach conclusions or to make official decisions, but to create a form of 'vacuum', towards which new ideas and energy are drawn and mixed. In this way the 'AFS-dices' are flipped over a couple of times more. I do not know on which side they will land, but I do know that the frustration and inspiration that I leave behind will trigger some kind of action.

The relation between strategic management and employees thus seems to be the reverse of that which prevailed in classic bureaucracy. Senior management does not provide rules or supply regulations, rather its main goal seems to have been to keep stable rules and regulations from forming, to 'keep the dices rolling' all of the time, to make sure that there is always 'vacuum'.

In the case of Skandia AFS it is apparent that the 'culture of trust' was not something that management provided for its employees. Rather the role of management was to prevent a stable cultural environment from forming; to generate insecurity, change, flux, to 'roll the dices', to simulate employees to continuously produce anew the relational and symbolic complexes that kept the organization together.

Skandia AFS might be an extreme example, but it illustrates the logic of corporate branding. Like product branding, organizational branding works by providing an ambience in which people are enabled or encouraged to *produce themselves* as members of the organization, and thereby produce the organization itself. What is subsumed is their capacity to produce a common: a context of action that subjectifies, that constructs and transforms their own selves. This is the reality behind the frequent management cliché about flexible organizations providing spaces for self-development. By creating a constant condition of mobility and insecurity, self-development is continuously put to work to generate the capacity for flexibility, for rapid and transitory local solutions, that is a key source of value for the organization.

Brand management as political entrepreneurship

In the form of brand management, capitalist governance has become immanently *political*. It works directly on what Hanna Arendt (1958) called 'action', the communicative construction of a web of stories, solidarities and identities that forms the basis for political passions and identification. Capital does this without the (previously) necessary mediation of the state. The Fordist model rested on the premises that the (bio)political reproduction of the workforce was to be achieved through the intervention of the state apparatus (Althusser, 1970). In part this was because the state, as a 'collective capitalist' could take on social costs that private entrepreneurs would refuse. In part it was to ensure that political passions and identification be channelled into the appropriate arena of parliamentary politics, and away from 'extremisms' (cf. Lipset, 1963). Today however, capital achieves this by itself, through the mechanism of the brand. Rather than the bodily effort of material labour, the brand subsumes the affective effort of immaterial labour, invested in the production of a common. The value of the brand thus builds on its capacity to appropriate identification with and attachment to the common: to appropriate *political* passions and affects. Politics ceases to be something separate from labour and consumption, from the domain of *oikos*, and (perhaps because of this) 'the political' (or at least the field of Fordist parliamentary politics) is loosing in autonomy and interest. As Paolo Virno puts it, 'there is already too much politics in wage labour for Politics to enjoy any autonomy or dignity of its own' (Virno, 2002: 43).

In the form of brand management, capital has discovered Lenin. Like Lenin, brand management understands that offering the possibility to *identify*, to become a subject, is crucial in order to mobilize and appropriate the energies of the social. Like Lenin, brand management works in a context where such opportunities are scarce; where older spaces of subjectivation – older communities and solidarities – are disappearing, and where new homeless classes emerge (in Lenin's case, the industrial proletariat; in the case of brand management, the new class of immaterial labour, the knowledge workers, the 'symbol analysts'). This way, brand management is a case of what Maurizio Lazzarato (1997) has called 'political entrepreneurship'. The term 'political entrepreneur' first surfaced with Max Weber in his essay on *Politics as a Vocation*. He used it to refer to people who *live off* politics in a systematic way: 'like the condottiere or the holder of a farmed-out or purchased office, or like the American boss who considers his costs a capital investment which he brings to fruition through exploitation of his influence' (Weber, 1948[1921]: 86; cf. Schumpeter, 1942). Political entrepreneurship is a matter of accumulating profits (or in any case a surplus), not through the direct exploitation of material labour, but through the exploitation of community, affect and communicative flows. To Lazzarato the brand is an example of political entrepreneurship extended to the domain of economics. The example he uses in his essay from 1997, Benetton, is a company that does not directly live off material labour. (The production of Benetton clothes is entirely out-sourced to third parties and beyond the company's direct control and responsibility.) Instead it lives off its brand. In turn, the brand is built through the accumulation of the attention, solidarity and affect generated by Benetton's customers (when confronted with one of the company's spectacular advertisements or when reading the magazine *Colors*), or otherwise solicited by the company's promotional activities. It also builds on Benetton's ability to directly 'breathe with the market' and rapidly accommodate supply to a shifting demand. (Cash registers in Benetton stores are connected to an information system that processes the data thus generated into production orders in Real Time. This way, the communicative interaction between customers in the stores – 'Red sweater or blue?' – is directly abstracted into market information that allows a flexibility which in turn raises the value of the brand.) Nike is a more contemporary example of the same principle. Material production is out-sourced and beyond the formal control of the company. Brand value is built through the appropriation of solidarity and affect generated in a plurality of different circumstances: in the Nikestore, on the sponsored inner-city basketball court, on the Nike Goddess website for women, through the surveillance of teenage tastes and, not least by the construction of the company itself as an ambience of identification that permits employees to produce themselves as appropriate Nike people. The value of the brand is based on the exploitation of a number of communicative and affectual processes that transpire among consumers and among employees. It is based on the ability to make the brand enter into social life and become an aspect of the relations, identities, fantasies, desires and hopes that social life generates. The ideal is sometimes to make the brand ubiquitous. Coca-Cola, the world's most valuable brand, prides itself on its success in this. As Ira Herbert, former marketing director of the Coca-Cola company described this strategy: 'the ideal outcome . . . is for consumers to see Coca Cola as woven into their local context, an integral part of their everyday world' (Curtin, 1996: 187).

This way, running Nike, Benetton or Coca-Cola is not very different from running a political organization – or, as van Ham (2001) suggests, a state. (And as Chapter 6 will discuss, brand value is usually estimated by some form of poll that measures the attention of consumers. This means that the goal of brand management becomes similar to that of everyday parliamentary politics: a good standing in the polls.) Given this convergence it is perhaps not strange that the values of brand management have re-entered political life proper. One of the most spectacular examples of this is Silvio Berlusconi's founding of a political party, *Forza Italia*, in 1994 and his subsequent electoral victory. Contrary to expectations, Berlusconi's party survived the demise of his first government in December 1994, won the elections in 2001 and has since presided over one of the most long-lived governments in Italian post-war history. Berlusconi's 1994 victory was contingent on the total collapse of the old Italian party system, following the *tangentopoli* corruption scandal in 1992 (where virtually all of the old political class was delegitimized). This left a mass of 'homeless' centre-right voters (the former Christian Democrat and Socialist electorate). It also posed a serious personal threat to Mr Berlusconi himself, as the very likely victory of the ex-communist-headed left alliance would definitely deprive him of the political support necessary to maintain his monopoly over private television and protect him from the many criminal proceedings in which he was involved. The success of *Forza Italia* (officially launched in late January 1994, the party acquired 21 per cent of the active electorate in the elections of 27 March) was certainly contingent on the existence of such a large homeless electorate that, like Mr Berlusconi felt 'the communist threat' (although perhaps less tangibly so; Berlusconi after all risked financial ruin and possibly a term in prison). But it also depended on Mr Berlusconi, and his company, Fininvest's skilful construction of a political brand.

To a large extent, *Forza Italia* capitalized on the identification of the

Italian middle classes with the commercial television channels that Berlusconi's company Fininvest had developed since the mid-1970s. In the face of a gradual decline of political and religious solidarities during the 1980s, these channels had spread a new cultural ideology of entre-preneurial global consumerism, with which many came to identify. (And which Berlusconi personified through his flamboyant riches and personal success story.) Indeed, Italian political scientist Ilvo Diamanti claimed that, without the personal image of Berlusconi and without the private television-networks through which it was sold, the *Forza Italia* product would not have had a market (Diamanti, 2003). *Forza Italia* was positioned in such a way that it appeared as the political expression of the cultural ideology of consumerism (Sklair, 1991) promoted by Fininvest's channels. That way, a commitment to, say, watching *Dallas* and visiting shopping centres (the 'Euromarkets' that Berlusconi had begun to launch in the early 1990s) could be translated into solidarity with a political project. Fininvest also constructed a pre-structured space for political involvement: the *Forza Italia* clubs. The movement of the clubs was orchestrated by top Fininvest managers and the first clubs emerged among Fininvest personnel and its clients (particularly the advertising clients of Publitalia, Fininvest's advertising concessionary). Although the first clubs were orchestrated from above, they soon began to develop spontaneously as news got around, mostly through Fininvest controlled media. The movement of the clubs developed rapidly to include, at the eve of the elections, almost 1 million members organized in some 14,000 clubs (according to Fininvest's own sources; others speak of half a million members organized in some 10,000 clubs; cf. Bardi, 1996). Any-one could form a club as long as he or she purchased a '*kit presidente*', consisting of a pin, a pen, a tie, a briefcase, a flag and a number of instruction videos on topics such as politics and economics, at the price of lire 250,000 (roughly $180 at the time). Club members had no influence on the political programme or strategy of the party. The party and the movement of the clubs were completely separated on the administrative level and there were no channels of communication between the two, neither did club members have any autonomous access to the media. The clubs rather served as a staged social movement, as a kind of brand-space where ordinary Italians could acquire the experience of political participation at the cost of a *kit presidente*, a 'do it yourself participation tool kit' (Paolucci and Barbesino, 1995: 15), and produce attention that could be mobilized into political capital through surveys, focus groups and other forms of political market research. As a political brand, *Forza Italia* did not represent any interest articulated from below. Rather, like any brand, it served as a vehicle by means of which political energies that had been set free could be mobilized to support a strategic project articulated at the top. This independence from articulated popular interest also meant that ideology became a matter of positioning. As in the case of brand management in general, *Forza Italia* used a number of techniques of market research to sculpt a message that would be as attractive for its target audience as possible. In 1994 this resulted in a general anti-system profile emphasizing newness and free markets, against the stale bureaucracy represented by the old party system. But since the political message was independent of popular participation (except indirectly as mediated through focus groups and opinion polls) it was also highly mobile. As any brand, the Forza Italia message developed over time, while retaining its core values. By 2001, Berlusconi's message had acquired more conservative, patriarchal and statesman-like qualities: he now presented himself as a sort of responsible national father figure (Ginsborg, 2004). The point is, however, that the ideological discourse of the party did not matter much. It had virtually no bearings on everyday politics. It was not even coherent. As Amadori catalogues, Berlusconi was in the habit of constantly contradicting himself: 'Berlusconi's political project is able to answer to the needs of everybody: who wants less taxes, who wants a job, who wants to be a success, who claims that everybody could be like Berlusconi' (Amadori, 2002). Amadori sees it as a sort of political extension of the fundamentally incoherent nature of the discourse of commercial 'neotelevision' where zapping and zipping forms a sort of mosaic between disparate images and soundbites. What counts is not the rational message so much as its emotional offer. Berlusconi's main rhetorical feat is what Amadori calls 'edulcrazione', *sweetening*. He is capable of presenting the world as a better, happier and sweeter place. Like McDonald's or Disney he offers this as a possible experience. As in the case of brand management, it is the emotional level that counts, the ability to appropriate affect. And the link to rationality or reality is severed. To Amadori, it does not matter if Berlusconi's political promises are not fulfilled as long as he can deliver a feeling with which people can identity. Similarly it does not matter how Nike's shoes are produced, as long as the promise that you can Just Do It, remains as a tangible experiential possibility.

Like commercial brands, the political brand is an answer to the homelessness of post-modern subjects. Like commercial brands it profits from this homelessness by offering a possibility for identification within a pre-structured space. This identification is generally framed, not in terms of rational interest, but in terms of emotional experiences. Indeed, brand management presupposes a scarcity of spaces where people can articulate their own rational understandings, where they can become self-conscious subjects in the modern sense.

Coda: interactivity and affect

The purpose of brand management is to guide the investments of affect on the part of consumers (or other subjects). This is true regardless of whether the brand refers to a consumer good, an organization or a political movement or party – or some combination of the above. In any case it is a matter of creating an affective intensity, an experience of unity between the brand and the subject. Brand management is about making the becoming of subjects and the becoming of value coincide. As in other instances where the creation of value is based on investments of affect, this process proceeds through the agency of subjects: it is an interactive process (Negri, 1999). This way, the difference between brand management and Fordist advertising can be captured well by the distinction between 'discipline' and 'interactivity' as general paradigms of governance, set up by Andrew Barry (2001: 149–50).

Discipline, Barry argues, provides a timetable: like the Fordist consumption norm constructed by means of advertising it works by prescribing particular times and places for particular activities. Brand management rather depends on the choice of the user as to the time, space, or general modality of interaction with the brand. Discipline, like the Fordist consumption norm, depends on the 'correlation of the body and the gesture', the creation of a subject that is able to focus on one particular pursuit, concentrate on the task at hand. Brand management presupposes 'an orientation of creative capacity', it 'depends on the potential of the undisciplined body and the unfocused mind', its ability to multi-task, move about in a complex environment and produce unexpected results. Discipline, like the Fordist consumption norm, produces enduring subjectivities, 'roles' through rules and codes that persist in time. Interactive brand management relies on the constitution of brief interaction and the maximization of their value. Discipline, like Fordist advertising relies on the authority of experts. In brand management 'the authority of the expert is partly hidden in order to maximize the possibilities for interaction'. Discipline says: *Learn! You Must!* Brand Management says: *Discover! You May!*

Conclusion

For consumers, brands are means of production. They function as a pre-established context of consumption that anticipates a certain style, mood or experience. This way brands can be employed to produce a particular kind of ethical surplus: a form of subjectivity (me and my Nikes), a social relation (me and my kids at McDonald's) or a shared experience. Brands are deployed in the ongoing *production* of a common sociality that characterizes post-modernity. The use-value of a brand rests on its utility as a means of production in that process.

For capital, brands are a means of appropriation. They are a way to capture the productivity of the social and subsume it as a form of value-generating immaterial labour. This is achieved in two ways. First, the productivity of vanguard groups is appropriated as it evolves spontaneously and is utilized as a source of innovation or product/brand development. Second, the productivity of ordinary consumers is posited so that it reproduces a given brand image. This is achieved by the provision of the brand as a biased platform for action. In working as a tool, the brand also pre-structures the productive process of consumers and makes it evolve in a particular direction. Contemporary brand management is distinguished by its extended intervention. It provides a space in which life – in turn empowered by its transpiring within the General Intellect of media culture – can become a direct source of value. Brands represent the transformation of the context for life into capital, and of life itself into labour, which is typical of informational capitalism. Brands are not just a new kind of interface between production and consumption, conceived in the classic sense. They are this too, but they are also a mechanism that tends to include consumption, the activities that underpin the social circulation of commodities, into the production process. Brands are a kind of de-territorialized factory where the productive mass intellectuality and the new forms of surveillance enabled by electronic media come together.

5 Online branding

The previous chapter began our investigation of contemporary brand management by looking at its most traditional form: the branding of consumer goods. I suggested that even here, where the brand is perhaps closest to its original role as a 'symbolic extension' of the object, its reference – what was actually branded – was not so much consumer goods themselves. Rather, the brand referred to a context of consumption, constructed by links between material objects, media discourses and life-world environments, and by accumulated consumer affect. This brand-space was furthermore open-ended and incomplete. It constituted a virtual promise or anticipation, to be actualized by the active involvement of consumers themselves. In their ongoing production of a common, consumers create the actual value of the brand: its share in meaningful experiences, its connection to social identities or forms of community: the practices that underpin measurable (and hence valuable) forms of attention. Brand management consists in a series of attempts to pre-structure or anticipate the kinds of actions that consumers perform around brands, and the meanings that they attribute to them. Furthermore, these attempts at governing through anticipation could be more or less detailed or strict. Brand management moves on a continuum from the highly structured brandscape or branded community where the whole environment serves to guide the consumer in a certain direction; via the 'politics of product placement', where a looser structure of expectations is created by inserting the brand in particular milieus; to, on the opposite extreme, the simple saturation of the life-world, paralleled by forms of overall macro surveillance, like trend-scouting or data mining.

All of these techniques, as well as the branding principle in general are taken one step further on the internet. In the 1990s internet enthusiasts, particularly those identified with the 'California ideology' often claimed that the internet will provide a kind of technological embodiment of the 'cultures of freedom' that came out of the 1960s; that its technological 'affordances' (Hutchby, 2001) foster new forms of non-hierarchical participatory engagement. To a certain extent this has proven to be true: part of the success of the internet can be explained by the fact that it offered a possibility to continue an originally political project – political in the sense of the politics of difference and community, of 'Life Politics' (Giddens, 1991) – with more efficient technological means: bulletin board systems (BBSs) and mailing list instead of video tapes and photocopied fanzines. To some extent new information and communication media have realized Enzenberger's (1970) old vision of a more participatory media culture. But the internet, particularly in its emerging mobile form, also shows a close technological fit with capital's strategic response to mass intellectuality: branding. First, digitization allows for an unprecedented plasticity and malleability of content (Manovich, 2001: 27). This means that content, the message, is radically separated from the medium that carries it. Immaterial content, like brands, can travel between different environments and across different media platforms (and as we have seen elsewhere this capacity for technological convergence is precisely what is now being exploited by the culture industries; cf. Hesmondhalgh, 2002; Murdoch, 2000). Content thus becomes environmental, rather than representational. It produces a milieu where particular forms of attention and sense making can unfold. Second, the internet has a capacity to absorb the subject (Murray, 1997). This capacity is unprecedented in its multidimensionality: it involves visual experience (as does cinema), but also sociality, communication and, in some games, also tactility and muscular response. Online computer games provide immersive environments that speak to many different senses, sight, hearing and tactility, and some research suggests that online communication has showed capable of fostering almost unprecedented levels of intimacy and openness (Bargh *et al.*, 2002; McKenna *et al.*, 2002; Parks and Floyd, 1996). Taken together, these qualities mean that the internet has the capacity to create all-encompassing environments centred around a particular brand; environments where all actions, where activity in general, is always already anticipated by the programme of the brand. ICTs have the technological potential to complete the real subsumption of life under capital, to the extent that the becoming of subjectivity and the becoming of value coincide. While offline branding struggles to valorize particular aspects of communicative interaction, the internet is a technological tool that permits a much more far-reaching subsumption of productive interaction.

The sociable medium

> The internet is the fabric of our lives. If information technology is the present-day equivalent of electricity in the industrial era, in our age the internet could be likened to both the electrical grid and the electric engine because of its ability to distribute the power of information throughout the entire realm of human activity.
>
> (Castells, 2001: 1)

Manuel Castells' enthusiastic opening lines of the sequel to his 1996 bestseller *The Information Age, The Internet Galaxy* (2001), give an adequate summary of what has become common sense in 'the information age'. The internet enriches our lives by saturating them with information. But, if by 'the power of information' Castells refers exclusively to the availability of texts, images and other informational objects, then his proposition is only half true. True, the internet does function, for some people in some instances, as a library, but for others, the enormous amount of the stuff that is available risks burying the interesting nuggets in mountains of trash. Indeed, recent studies of the use of information technology suggest that the 'power of information' refers to something else, namely the ability to co-ordinate the communicative retrieval, interpretation and elaboration of information. The internet is useful as it serves as a tool that can be, and is employed in the collective production of knowledge, and other immaterial goods, as much as it is useful as a retrieval device for already formulated pieces of information. (A recent survey shows that as much as 44 per cent of the American internet population have contributed, if sporadically, to the production on online content; Terdiman, 2004.) Indeed, this extended definition of 'the power of information' does not seem far-fetched to Castells. On the next page he goes on to explain the historical role of information technologies as that of providing precisely the unprecedented capacities of co-ordination that enable unstructured forms of 'network sociality' to take precedence over the hierarchical organizations of industrial modernity.

> The introduction of computer-based information and communication technologies, and particularly the Internet, enables networks to deploy their flexibility and adaptability, thus asserting their evolutionary nature. At the same time, these technologies allow the coordination of tasks and management of complexity.
>
> (Castells, 2001: 2)

The 'evolutionary superiority' gained by 'the net', or more precisely information and communication technologies come with the capacity, or better *bias* of the medium towards non-hierarchical, co-operative coordination. This rests principally with two of its fundamental technological properties: the network architecture and interactivity. Network architecture, originally developed for military purposes, makes it very difficult to maintain a centralized control over the communicative flows on the net. There is simply no privileged position from which a master command function can be exercised. Rather, the authority to command and control must be enforced by other means. Interactivity refers to a basic feature of digitized media in general; they allow for or even sometimes require that users elaborate, respond to or act in relation to the messages that they display (Manovich, 2001). Insofar as computers are networked, and messages originate with another actor, this interactivity becomes both technological (in the sense of human–machine interaction) and sociological (in the sense of human–human interaction; Jensen, 1999). Some networked ICTs, like those commonly found in the public domain of the internet can thus posit people as participants in a non-hierarchical communication process that enables (and sometimes encourages) them to respond, by acting on, elaborating or manipulating the messages they receive. (In other instances, as in private domains like corporate intranets, the subject positions of users can be quite different.) These properties cater to the emergence and maintenance of emergent social formations that can develop and function without any pre-given structural script. Manuel Castells argues that the fit between the mediatic properties of computer-mediated communication technologies and the sociological requirement of a capitalism in need of restructuring explains the rapid implementation of these technologies in business life.

I think the same can be said for another important factor behind the development of what we today refer to as the internet, the grassroots computer activism of the early 1980s. In their first manifestations early networks like Blacksburg Electronic Village, Cleveland Freenet and FIDONET were continuations of the new, emergent forms of sociality that had grown out of the 1960s counter-culture, in particular in its manifestation on university campuses. The San Francisco based WELL, one of the most important gathering points for early ICT enthusiasts, was heavily populated by 'deadheads' or members of the Grateful Dead fan-culture; in Europe, projects like the 'Amsterdam Free City' or the Italian 'Decoder' grew out of squatter and 'autonomist' movements of the 1970s (Rheingold, 1993; Castells, 2001). To a large extent the early grassroots developments of what was to become the internet were driven by users appropriating new media technologies and using them for their own, often politically motivated purposes. A similar kind of 'art of practice' (de Certeau, 1984) also prevailed among many of the computer scientists and engineers who worked to build the official architecture of the network.

Many of them embraced a vision of the 'net' as an open-ended 'cooking pot market' (Ghosh, 1999) or 'high-tech gift economy' (Barbrook, 1999) devoted to the production of commonly available use-values without direct monetary awards (Himanen, 2001; Harries, 2002). Indeed, at least until its growing commercialization in the 1990s, many of the innovations that today seem most important were the result of users appropriating technology and using it for their own purposes. Often these purposes would involve 'non-productive' forms of sociability, like gossip, the exchange of ephemeral material or pure procrastination. Email, one of the earliest applications behind what was to become the internet, grew out of the ability to exchange technical messages built into ARPANET, the computer network developed for purposes of military communication and the sharing of supercomputer resources. Soon, however, users began to employ email for purposes that went far beyond professional communication, and internet mailing lists devoted to ephemeral topics like science fiction began to materialize (Blasi, 1999; Hardy, 1993). Usenet, the first major structure outside ARPANET was developed in 1979 by students at Duke University and devoted to discussion groups. Usenet was administered by the users themselves, and in the absence of centralized control, the threat of flaming worked as the main disciplinary sanction. Here, the emergence of the alt domain, devoted to saucier subjects like sex and drugs was a response to ARPANET administrators initially refusing to carry discussion groups on sex. Interested users simply invented alternative routings largely avoiding the ARPANET computers, hence 'alt' for 'alternative'. In developing these early structures users employed the fixed capital supplied by universities and government bureaucracies, and, not least, the labour time formally appropriated by these institutions. Not only was early software development largely the work of people otherwise paid to be university faculty or maintained as students, but many others engaged in communicative interaction during their work hours when they were presumably paid to do something else. Richard Sexton, one of the actors behind the emergence of the alt.sex domain provides a good example of this in his anecdotic account of events.

> It was a warm sunny 1988 afternoon in Baldwin Park, California. I was working at Lundy Financial Systems, who made remittance processing robots. While everybody else was playing with the neat cool groovy next generation UNIX machines, I was contracted to fix the 8 year old Z-80/Assembler coded behemoth that nobody else would touch. It was a horrible job. Mind numbing does not begin to describe it. With such a job like this, there was only one thing to do: read talk.bizarre for 7 hours a day.
>
> (Sexton, 1995)

At least to some extent, the emergence of the new technology was driven by attempts to avoid the rigours and boredom of paid work. During the 1980s the proliferation of personal computers and the emergence of structures like BitNet, FidoNet, commercial providers like AOL, Compuserve and Prodigy, and state provided services like the French Minitel, permitted the large-scale dedication of time subtracted from work, leisure and family life to the production of social and symbolic bonds around a wide variety of issues. The internet became an autonomous area that had grown within the technospace of capital, built though various forms of free labour – unpaid and unsupervised (Terranova, 2004: 79; Tapscott, 1996). Knowledge and sociality could form around topics that had previously been either marginalized or restricted to the domains of private life or leisure, like consumer information and gardening, political causes and emotional issues and sexual interests. It would also mobilize groups that had previously been silent: housewives, for example, were one significant group of such early users (Cherny and Wese, 1996; cf. Rheingold, 1993; Baym, 1996; Dibbel, 1997; Kollock and Smith, 1996; Putnam, 2000). In this sense, a significant part of what is today known as the internet has evolved as part of a technologically extended mass intellectuality, supplying a set of techniques and capacities to be employed in the more or less unrestricted production of sociality.

Online brand management

> We must stop thinking of ICT as a medium for managing information: To say that the internet is about information is the same as saying that cooking is about oven temperature – right, but wrong. The real creator of value is relationships.
>
> (Schrage, 1997)

When the branding literature began to take the challenge of ICTs seriously, sometime in the mid-1990s, the conditions posed by 'the net' were generally read as a technological embodiment of those prevailing in 'post-modern consumer societies' in general. In particular, it was supposed that 'consumers on the net' are active, reflexive and that they crave 'interactivity'. The internet, most agree, has put an end to the 'classic' or Kotlerian approach to marketing. Then, brand identity and advertising messages were elaborated by brand managers and communicated to consumers who passively absorbed (or rejected) the message. Now, consumers are empowered and interactive and should be invited to participate in the elaboration of the brand, as well as the product or service that they purchase. (As previous chapters have shown, such thoughts are not new or exclusive to the 'Information Age'. But marketing professionals generally have very short memories.) In the internet environment successful brands are those that involve consumers (McWilliam, 2000). Thus recommendations for the design of company web pages often recommend architectures that stimulate consumer interaction. On the web, where attention is scarce, 'competition is just a click away' and consumers are empowered by their access to information and market choice, it is vital to cater to their demand for interactive 'experiences', in order to make them stick around or even come back (Norton and Hansen, 2001; Schmitt, 2000). Indeed, 'the internet is not about transactions, it's about dialogue and relationships' and 'what fascinates consumers is the quality of the dialogue he or she can engage in' (Ind and Rondino, 2001: 14–15). Hence the Web's most popular site in 2000, BritneySpears.com, owed much of its popularity to the interactive forum that it supplied, Britney's World, where adolescent fans (and the occasional dirty old man in disguise, one suspects) could exchange information on and create social ties around the life and deeds of their idol. Procter & Gamble use a similar strategy for the online marketing of their sanitary product Always. Their website Always.com comes in a number of country-specific versions aimed at US, Canadian, South American and Scandinavian markets. Its different sections give advice to mothers and teenage girls entering puberty and experiencing the accompanying transformations of their bodies and sexual attitudes. The site gives advice for mothers and recommends on topics of discussion that can be used in informing daughters about the new issues that they are facing. Similarly, it suggests how daughters might want to deal with their parents. All of these advice columns have sections directly devoted to the choice of sanitary products. Furthermore, an interactive forum,

BeingGirl.com is directed at teen and pre-teen girls. It offers them a chance to share experiences about their bodies, their sexuality or their social life in general. It also features articles and various forms of interactive material (like self-discovery quizzes) devoted to these topics as well as to things like school, dieting and peer pressure. The idea behind the site is that engagement in community-like interaction will generate emotional and experiential ties that will, in turn, have an effect on the status of the brand in the minds of consumers, and consequently, the equity of the Always brand. Similarly, amazon.com fosters a 'community of book lovers' where users are encouraged to write reviews and share book recommendations with each other. E-bay lets users rate each other, thus creating both an ingenious way of generating trust and offering a community experience where trusted users can enjoy the status they have accumulated in the eyes of others. Another way to involve consumers is to invite them to participate in the design or customization of the product or service purchased. Nike enables consumers to personalize the design of their shoes, including adding on personal text messages. (This function was famously spoofed in 2000 by journalist and media activist Jonah Peretti. He demanded a pair of sneakers with 'Sweatshop' written on them. Nike refused. His request and subsequent conversation with Nike was widely circulated on the web, employing the techniques of viral marketing against the branding giant; cf. Peretti, 2001.) Reflect.com invite customers to design their own cosmetics, in interaction with the '7000 international scientists' present on the site (virtually, one assumes). The customization process not only promises to produce superior cosmetics, but also offers consumers a chance to experience their own personal uniqueness – neatly summarized in the *non sequitur* 'Because you are an individual, we believe you can only be satisfied with products made uniquely for you.' In this function, the process of actually designing cosmetics is supported by a wealth of interactive content; mainly tests and questioners that touch on personal and emotional issues. Designing cosmetics also becomes a process of interactive self-discovery, a process in which fantasy can be put to work in the production of a self. Similarly, toy manufacturer Lego's sub-brand Bionicle offers games and message boards that are routinely surveyed by designers to find fresh inputs to be used in the product development process. Here part of the production of new products as well as the overall story within which the brand evolves are socialized and made to evolve through customer interaction (Brickner, 2002). Car manufacturers like Volvo, Peugeot and Audi have used Community Based Innovation (CBI) initiatives to involve people who frequent their websites in the process of designing and elaborating future models (Fuller *et al.*, 2004). These sites continue and expand the tradition of Customer Relationship Management, pioneered in the 1980s, by aiming to construct 'deep relationships' with consumers, hoping that thus expanding the transaction into an experience that meets 'multiple social and commercial needs' might be the key to success in the online environment (Hagel and Armstrong, 1997: 5; cf. Andrejevic, 2002).

So far, marketing efforts on the internet seem to conform to what has sometimes been termed the 'Nirvana Theory' of the information economy, propagated by the likes of Bill Gates (1996) and Nicolas Negroponte (1995). Here, the general idea is that the internet environment offers a kind of 'frictionless' capitalism in which transaction costs approach zero and ubiquitous and free information increases the power of consumers relative to marketers or 'vendors'. As Hagel and Armstrong, two McKinsey consultants, put it in their early book on the commercial challenge posed by the mass intellectuality of the internet (they are worth quoting at length as they neatly sum up what goes for the prevailing wisdom):

> In their relationships with customers, vendors have long held the upper hand. This has to do with information. Access to information is a key determinant of bargaining power in any commercial trans-action. If one party gains access to more information, that party tends to be able to extract more value from transactions than a party with access to less information. In most markets today, vendors are armed with comparatively more information than their customers . . ..
> Virtual communities are likely to turn these market dynamics upside down by creating 'reverse markets' – markets in which the customer, armed with a growing amount of information, uses that information to search out vendors offering the best combination of quality and price tailored to his or her individual needs' . . .. In fact the ability to access more information, and thereby extract more value from vendors will ultimately be one of the major incentives drawing members into virtual communities.
>
> (Hagel and Armstrong, 1997: 17)

In the future that they envisioned in 1997, 'reverse markets' will make it increasingly difficult for vendors to exploit their traditional information monopoly, hence pushing prices downwards and quality upwards as consumers will no longer settle for less than full satisfaction. This vision of the internet as an environment where capitalism could finally become democratic, approaching its textbook version as supply and demand curves clear out at a price and quantity that satisfies everybody's preferences, was dear to the commercial pioneers of the dot.com era. It has since come to clash with a more mature information capitalism that shows a more Braudelian nature. Braudel's (1985) point about capitalism was that it was not the same as free markets, but rather the opposite to free markets. To him, the essence of capitalism is the restriction of free exchange through practices of market control and monopoly. The Napster case is perhaps the most well known example of the crucial nature that the restriction of free exchange continues to play within informational capitalism (McCourt and Buckhart, 2003). This tendency is rooted in the central dynamic of informational capitalism, in which content becomes the key strategic resource (Preston, 2000; Todreas, 1999). The valorization of content presupposes its monopolization, in some form, or at least the existence of measures that restrict its circulation. But because the technological means employed to valorize content also permit, or even encourage its free circulation, such monopolization becomes inherently problematic. Indeed, the economics of content manifests an emerging contradiction within informational capitalism: between means and relations of production. Because of this new value of monopolized content, internet branding is evolving into a series of techniques that aim to put consumers to work in the production of forms of content that can be sold back to them. The brand becomes the institutional form by means of which capital brings the free labour of the internet back into its fold. In this form, the internet is no longer conceived as a means towards the valorization of an otherwise independent product or service. Rather, it is conceived as a economic space in its own right, an arena for both the production and the consumption of branded content. The medium becomes a technological extension of the brand-logic. Two important examples of this putting to work of users themselves are online interactive gaming and internet dating.

Branding sociality

The transformation of user activity into commodified content emerged as one of the earliest strategies for making money on the internet. Early providers like AOL attempted to do this, rather rudimentarily, through their 'walled garden' strategy, in which access to 'content' – websites and discussion groups on the AOL domain – was contingent on paying a user's fee. As the internet advertising/audience market has developed, however, many sites have come to rely on more targeted strategies.

Instead of AOL's catch-all approach, they have positioned themselves as representative of a particular kind of content, and of a particular kind of user. For example, Epinions (that has now merged with DealTime into Shopping.com) not only provides customer reviews and opinions, but *trustworthy* customer opinion. Indeed, for DealTime, it was this trustworthy nature of Epinions customer advice that motivated the take-over: 'Epinions has a reputation as a trustworthy source of consumer advice . . .. By contrast many of the reviews currently published on DealTime (and most of the other shopping search engines for that matter) appear to be posted by shills, over-hyping products or retailers, or publishing unrealistically negative criticisms' (Sherman, 2003). In the case of Epinions, this 'genuine trust' was produced by users themselves. Epinions does not operate any overall control or censorship to guarantee the trustworthy user postings. Indeed, 'Epinions is a platform for people to share their experiences' (www.epinions.com/about). However, a clever device called the 'web of trust' achieves this goal by putting to work a quality often observed in online communication: that it tends to constitute users as members of a community.

In his ethnographic work on 'sexpics' trading on IRC, Don Slater observed this mechanism at work. Although the sexpics traded were infinitely reproducible and hence without exchange value, traders went to great lengths to establish price relations and to punish 'lechers' and others who downloaded content without offering anything in return. Sexpics traders constructed a purely ethical economy without any material base (Slater, 1998). Slater suggests that these efforts were triggered precisely by the absence of such a material (or 'embodied') base to the exchange:

> I will argue that although, or because, the 'sexpics' scene problematized materiality – and indeed probably more than most other Internet settings – participants went to great lengths to make 'things' material (the objects they traded, their trading partners and the transactions themselves). They set in motion a considerable range of 'mechanisms of materialization', and they did so in order to establish a sense of ongoing ethical sociality.
>
> (Slater, 2002: 227)

Students of other kinds of online communication have reached similar results. Many, and in particular earlier, enthusiastic students of 'cyberspace' have pointed at the emancipating potential of the kinds of disembodiments that it offers. At last, they hope, it will be possible to engage in open-ended forms of sociality where powerful social categories like race, gender and sexuality no longer matter (cf. Featherstone and Burrows eds, 1995; Plant, 1997; Turkle, 1996)! There is of course a substantial grain of truth to such propositions. The internet with its absence of given bodily cues, offers a 'third space' where social relations can be playfully constructed, often involving a fair amount of lying and mutual fantasy (Whitty and Carr, forthcoming). But at the same time, it seems that users exploit the cues that are available (or invent new ones) to construct embodiments that anchor the interactive situation in some form of (however imaginary) 'materiality', or at least this is the case with more enduring relationships (Whitty and Carr, forthcoming; Donn and Sherman, 2002). Indeed, users have sometimes been shown to create significant emotional investments in their online identities, and to be deeply hurt when people they have developed enduring online relationships with are revealed as lying, or as Dibbel (1997) has chronicled in a famous early article, when their online identity is subjected to virtual abuse (cf. Rehak, 2003; Slater, 1998).

Almost regardless of the subject of the discussion at hand, be this the virtues of toasters or the exchange of pornographic images, online communication thus tends to produce a 'double' in the form of a more or less imagined communitarian order. Participants begin to regard other participants as parts to an ethical order, a 'community', and they begin to care about their standing, reputation or 'cred' in the face of others. This is precisely the mechanism that Epinions puts to work. The site not only lets users mark their trust and distrust of other users, but will 'go to great lengths to highlight the people behind the reviews', letting users publish biography pages and information on their general expertise and ability to comment. Users are thus given ample space to create online self-presentations and to comment on and communicate with those of others. Their desire for embodiment, or at least for the fundaments of ethical order, is thus stimulated and given a space to evolve. The 'web of trust' is a device that both empowers the ethical dimension of user interaction, and makes it work towards the aims of the brand. People's ability and desire to create and maintain meaningful relations is put to work to create its distinctive value. To thus 'put community to work' has been a conscious strategy on the part of the people behind Epinions, as in the case of amazon.com and E-bay (Regan, 2002).

One of the most important recent examples of this putting to work and commercial valorization of ICT-enhanced mass intellectuality are Massive Multiplayer Online Role Playing Games (or MMORPGs). MMORPGs are similar to the MUDs (Multi User Dungeons) that pioneered interactive online role-playing in the early 1990s. But they are much larger both in terms of the 'size' of the environments that they provide (*Ultima Online* has 'more than 189 million square feet of virtual surface' that users can roam around in; Wolf, 2001: 27), and in terms of the number of players that they attract. (A MMORPG becomes 'Massive' when it has more than 1,000 players, each represented by one or more avatars.) While MUDs generally used text interfaces, MMPORGs often have very detailed graphics. Most importantly perhaps, most MUDs were non-commercial sites, or at least they originated that way, while MMPORGs are commercial ventures, backed by big corporations (Sony runs *Everquest*, Microsoft runs *Asherons Call*, Electronic Arts runs *The Sims Online*), and they require massive investments in server space and personnel (Nuttall, 2003; Terdiman, 2004). Participating in one of these online worlds generally requires purchase of the game, and often some kind of subscription fee as well. One then registers and chooses an avatar, the personality that one wants to play in the game. The process of constructing an avatar generally involves quite a range of choices, but these choices are constrained by the environment of the particular game. Thus on *Everquest*, one can chose between a number of more or less fantastic occupations and 'species' (human, elf, *kyv*, *ukun*, and so on) and one can pick different qualities (physichal strength, intelligence, charisma, and so on), but it is impossible to be, for example, an African-American car mechanic (Rehak, 2003). Similarly, the Sims Online, that unfolds in a universe similar to that of an affluent North American middle class suburb, and not in a medieval/science fiction fantasy land like *Everquest*'s 'Norrath', provides a range of choices between characters that are distinctly middle class in outlook, orientation and appearance. All characters are perfect consumers for whom material possessions convert directly into happiness. (The purpose of the Sims is to make your chosen characters prosper. You do not play them yourself; instead you play God.) As the game unfolds, the avatars interact with others and solve different quests individually or collectively. As they gain experience, their skill, riches and other kinds of endowments increase. What they do also affects and leaves traces in the virtual world. An enriched player can, for example, build a castle or set up a business. In this sense MMPORGs are collectively produced worlds where player interaction continuously constructs the environment in which it unfolds. Users produce the content – in the form of a materialized, or 'virtualized' ethical surplus – that then becomes the true source of value for the owners of the game. Says Philip Rosedale, chief executive of Linden Lab, owners of the online virtual world Second Life: 'the value delivered is in the content created, the groups created and the social architectures created by the people inside the environment' (Terdiman, 2004). The trick, however, is to make users produce the right kind of content. The main way to achieve this is to make the branded environment supplied by the game-owners direct and limit the productive sociality that unfolds within its boundaries. Of course, restrictions can be implemented through policing: certain actions might lead to warnings or exclusions. (In the recruitment oriented multi-person shooter game *America's Army* – not really a MMOPRG – killing your own leads to suspension and ultimately, the termination of one's account.) Usually though, freedom is directed by the particular features of the environment. The outlay of the graphical environments, the fiction that gives coherence to the universe, the skills and qualities of characters and of the physical milieu, provide an artificial universe, a 'smooth space' where only certain kinds of actions are possible (cf. Pole, 2000). So MMPORGs are collectively produced realities, but this collective production process is in turn guided, restrained and empowered, in short, governed, by the restrictions and possibilities offered by the environment. In this way, MMORPGs are an example of how the interaction of users is put to work in ways that give it a particular direction; how it is governed 'from below' through the 'bio-political' environment in which it evolves. Commercial success then hinges on the ability to monopolize the valorization of user productivity. Often this is a matter of boring and burdensome tasks like those involved in training to acquiring the skills necessary to make one's avatar progress, like:

> producing impressive statistics through burdensome training (which often consists in nothing but the boring clicking of the same mouse button, or the carrying out of simple commands) . . .. The efforts put into developing a game character need not be the opposite of what happens in everyday life. Many games contain dull actions that make gaming similar to living.
>
> (Terdiman, 2004)

This activity can sometimes be a matter of rather massive inputs in time and energy (not to speak of connection fees). De Graaf and Nieborg (2003) cite the following estimate for *America's Army*:

> Game US as of November 16, 2002 saw 1,007,000 registered accounts, 614,000 graduates of basic rifle marksmanship and combat training (BCT) [going through this course is the first step to a 'career'

in the game], and more than 32 million missions completed (averaging 6 to 10 minutes). Missions per day average 338,380, with players typically accomplishing 21 missions after BCT. Assuming 10 minutes per mission, we calculate gamers racked up a combined 263 years of non-stop play in the first 58 days [of the game] alone . . .. To put it another way, if these hours were payable at minimum wage ($6.75 an hour), the bill would hit $15,590,367 for 58 days. And if we project the 4.6 years of play per day to 1,670 years of play per annum, we are looking at $99,279,270 of intensive effort donated gratis by America's youth.

(de Graff and Nieborg, 2003: 326)

This calculus might seem excessive. But, since the game began it has increased the flow of US army recruits by 28 per cent. (*America's Army* is not a commercial game, but its purpose is to act as a recruitment tool for the Army.) Given that the US army's annual recruitment costs reach $2 billion, the game can be said to have generated a revenue of $560 million. This translates into a net profit of at least $540 million (the game cost $7 million to develop: let's add on $1.3 million annually in maintenance costs – although this is probably excessive). Even if these figures are extra-ordinary, they hint at why the ability to monopolize and *privatize* the results of the collective production of users are crucial to commercial success. Recently, this imperative has led owners of MMORPGs, like Sony, into conflict with users who have specialized in developing characters and then selling them on internet auction sites like e-Bay. Since developing a character requires time (that users have to pay for) such practices obviously undermine the owner's monopoly over the content produced on the site. Selling a ready made character or a house or a set of skills means selling the results of one's investments in online time, duly paid for through subscription fees. Recently this practice has spurred a number of conflicts between users and game owners, as to the ownership of the game characters and game paraphernalia that users have built up during their time online (Taylor, 2003).

Another increasingly important example of the same principle of brand-governance is online dating. The internet dating sector has grown enormously over recent years. It encompasses a range of mainstream sites, like Match.com, Kiss.com, Matchmaker.com and Yahoo's Club Connect, as well as more niche-oriented operations like Eharmony (devoted to upscale singles), fitnessdate.com, Jdate.com (for Jewish singles) or alt.com, gathering people searching for partners to engage in specialized sexual practices. In addition, there are a plethora of geographically specific sites, like Eurosingles.com or the Danish Dating.dk. Many of the larger operations show very solid economics. Lavalife, a Canadian based site claims a total client base of 2 million in 2001, adding on 7,000 new customers *per day*. Together they produced a revenue of $100 million. Match.com, the largest operation, claimed 9 million registered members world-wide (7 million in the United States) and some 700,000 paying subscribers. In 2001 Ticketmaster (the company that owns match.com) reported that the site generated $16.5 million in earnings before interests, taxes, depreciation and amortization, on a revenue of $49.2 million. In 2002 it was estimated that 15 million US residents used the internet to find a partner. The figure is expected to rise to 24 million by 2007 (Graham, 2003). All in all, industry analysts claim the dating market is worth close to $1 billion (Olijnyk, 2002). There are of course many public venues on the internet where one can meet a partner, like chat-rooms, IRC, mailing lists or non-commercial dating sites. But commercial dating sites usually offer something extra – a branded embodiment. The branded environment guides and, this at least is the claim, facilitates the dating process; it offers security (the potential dangers of internet dating are constantly pointed at by commercial dating sites who all offer elaborate routines for establishing contacts and proceeding from the virtual to the actual); and, most importantly, it offers a particular brand of singles. On Match.com one meets Quality Singles, on eHarmony the kinds of singles who are truly ready for a long-term commitment, and so on. Here as well, the trick is to engage users in the kinds of social interaction that produces a desirable form of content. The site must make users present themselves and interact in ways that conform to the branded profile. As in the case of MMORPGs this can be achieved through censorship and policing. Match.com, for example, does not tolerate postings or profiles (the dating version of avatars) that contain 'abusive language, vulgarity, racism', 'discussions or descriptions of illegal acts of behaviour', the solicitation of additional partners (a Quality Single is monogamous) and 'over-sexual innuendo or discussion'. Furthermore, Match.com does not accept postings from 'individuals under the age of 18' and 'incarcerated individuals' (who are not Quality Singles!). Photographs are not accepted if they contain 'nude, obscene, sexual or otherwise offensive' material. Profiles are regularly reviewed and checked by a quality assurance team to ensure that these guidelines are accepted. Other sites can have different rules that are more or less stringent (more sexually explicit sites, like alt.com naturally has a higher tolerance of 'obscene material'), but all police user communication. Most importantly, however, most dating sites offer a branded environment that anticipates a particular style or attitude.

Relying on the fact that users crave a 'materiality', the brand offers a partial embodiment that reduces the complexity of the situation for users, and empowers romantic communication in a particular direction. As in the case of offline branding this is often done through a 'politics of product placements' that anchors the brand-space in media culture by establishing a series of intertextual linkages. In turn, these supply a milieu that anticipates a certain bundle of tastes and attachments; a certain *habitus*. Match.com, for example, has created a series of linkages and co-branding efforts. Many of these, like partnerships with Yahoo, Msn.com, AOL, Compuserve and Netscape where match.com offers its search engine and database in exchange for exposure, serve primarily to enlarge the customer base. This is also the case for Bet.com and Univision that provides a presence in the black and Hispanic middle class market. But they also craft out a position for the brand. Other linkages are more explicitly directed at profiling, as in the case of the Village Voice, Starbucks and Oxygen.com: the television station that features the Oprah Winfrey show (Blackett and Russell, 2000). Oxygen.com links to match.com on a site frequented by Oprah Winfrey's audience. Oprah, in turn has repeatedly endorsed match.com (as has Dr Phil on his show) and Oxygen.com launches a television show, eLove, that follows up on couples who have met on the internet. Similarly, Alex Michel, one time winner of the reality game show *The Bachelor* endorses Match.com and offers advice to prospective daters. Television spot, *True Stories*, that follows the talk show format featuring real life couples who met on Match.com, also serves to stress how the Oprah-style talk show genre, with its accompanying discourse of love and intimacy is one significant referent for the Match.com brand. (Match.com powers the personals section of John Gray, Ph.D.'s relationship site MarsVenus.com, and Gray, Ph.D.'s and Oprah's self-actualization ideology of relationships and love is largely replicated on the advisory material posted on Match.com, often with references back to Oprah and Gray, Ph.D.) The other significant pool of the brand image is the urban Single Girl image, as elaborated in shows like *Sex and the City*, largely replicated in Match.com's 'Single N'Happy' ad. This complex is also catered to by Match.com's brand extension, MatchLive, which targets a younger, urban crowd. MatchLive organizes social events for singles in major cities like New York, San Francisco, Los Angeles, Boston, Chicago and, recently, London. MatchTravel organizes singles vacations for the same target. Here as well the kinds of activities offered are aimed at a particular life-style. In May 2003, for example, MatchLive in New York offers a guided tour of Central Park, an evening at a Hawaiian lounge bar ('You'll want to come out for this night of pure Tikki kitsch'). In San Francisco, MatchLive offers an evening at the theatre, a night of Argentine tango, and a kayaking excursion, wine tasting and a sushi course. In London it's a Salsa evening, a Champagne Party and a picnic at the Chelsea flower market. (This last event is co-branded with the Oddbins chain of wine stores.) MatchTravel offers Carribean holidays, a biking tour of Tuscany, a trip to New York and a cruise to Alaska. These activities are co-branded with ClubMed (that in turn offered a single's vacation in Cancun, Mexico, featuring Alex Miller the 'survivor' of the previous season's *Bachelor* game show). In short, these brand extensions anticipate a *habitus* that is distinctly middle class, middle-brow and mainstream.

This anticipated habitus translates into a real embodiment through the registration process. This is, in effect, a process of self-branding, in which the insecurities that most users feel before constructing a potentially successful online profile are met with guidelines that give this process a very particular direction. Since this is effectively the situation where users produce content for the site, in the form of profile that other users can browse through and even contact, users are encouraged to devote a significant amount of intellectual energy to the elaboration of a profile. Generally, this process is time consuming, involving answers to a large number of questions and the provision of little essays. (eHarmony has the record here, requiring users to answer 500 questions covering the 21 dimensions of compatibility with which its 'scientific matching' service operates.) Match.com advises that 'Your personal should reflect what makes you uniquely you'. Users are encouraged to 'describe your match in distinctive terms' and to 'avoid broad terms that are basically meaningless and could describe anyone'. Such creativity is presented to be in the best interest of users. A bland profile 'makes you seem lazy at best, insincere at worst' (Lester, 2003). The ways in which they can freely express and present themselves are however rather strictly guided by the environment. Upon registering, users are asked to describe themselves by answering a series of multiple choice questions on topics like Hair Colour, Eye Colour, Body Type, Ethnicity, Education, Occupation and Income, possession of or interest in children. The site encourages people to answer these questions as thoroughly as possible: they provide a 'quick sketch of who you are, your lifestyle and what counts most in a relationship'. This information also serves to feed to the site's search engine, Venus, which provides compatible profiles on a weekly or even daily basis. Already at entering and registering the site communicative agency is empowered in such ways that contribute to the provision of desirable content. This shaping of communicative action into content proceeds all through the registration process. In the next step users are asked to provide more personal information about themselves through another set of structured questions and through a short, 100–200 word self-description. Here too, the questions shape the self-presentation according to the particular Quality Singles genre that the site represents. Users are encouraged to take a kind of parlour game approach to self-presentation answering questions like 'What is your ideal place to live?' (A loft in the city/A house in the suburbs/A cottage in the country and so on). Further questions regard attitudes to cleanliness, sense of fashion, sense of humour, taste in music, pets and more general 'Turn Ons and Turn Offs' (like tattoos, body piercings, long hair, and so on). If at a loss for words when describing themselves – this is recognized to be the difficult part – users are provided with a set of questions to help them reflect. These largely fall into areas of interest particular to Match.com's brand of Quality Singles, like shopping, hobbies, tastes in fun and the Oprah Winfrey kind of 'spirituality and self-actualization' discourse that Match.com embraces: 'What makes you proud?'; 'What makes you at peace?'

Generally Match.com directs the focus of romantic discourse away from 'material' things like income, social status or physical attraction (which are anyway easy to manipulate in the online environment that they provide). It abstracts away from the Real Life situation of users. Instead, it encourages its users to focus on the 'spiritual side'; values, ideals and beliefs (of which it is perhaps easier to have a meaningful conversation with people whose social determination, or embodiment is unsure). The process of registering at Match.com and creating a user profile entails adaptation to a certain streamlined 'language' or communication style that resonates with the image of the Quality Single that Match.com represents and sells. The site very cleverly utilizes the awkwardness many users might feel in front of the medium (how does one write a romantically successful self-presentation on the internet?) to guide and shape those presentations in ways that conform to the kind of Quality Single that the site represents.

Sociality on the internet can be defined as a kind of communicative fantasy. You cannot see the other, but he or she leaves clues that you have to fill in by imagining. (Of course, this is true in face-to-face communication too, but there, material presence and bodily clues make a difference.) As you communicate, this fantasizing becomes mutual and communicative. Together you imagine each other, your relationship, what you could do together. MMOPRGs and dating sites are both 'places' where this capacity for communicative imaginings is put to work. In MMOPRGs participants build a world out of pure fantasy. In dating games, they build online relationships – romantic or erotic – that do not necessary have to evolve towards real life contact. In putting the imagination to work, both these kinds of places generally guide it towards the production of a certain form of content. To some extent this is done through policing. But, for the most part, guidance happens from below: by providing a partial embodiment in the form of an interaction-space, a particular kind of avatar or a particular kind of language, that makes it more likely that a particular kind of content is produced. The brand space serves to provide this partial embodiment: it anticipates a certain set of actions and attitudes. In online environments such as these, this anticipation can be more far-reaching than in Real Life, as the brand serves to provide a total space that not only surrounds the user but also partially constitutes his or her online personality. Indeed, it is illustrative that many dating sites have developed links to Reality television. Like the Reality show, these sites produce content by situating participants in environments that are artificial (in the sense of being purposely built) total, and empowering. Like the boys and girls on Robinson's island, Match.com users move in a world where the possibilities and limitations of action as well as problems and opportunities are local, specific and all encompassing. Indeed, you can argue that the Reality genre illustrates (or perhaps better, celebrates) a particular way of putting subjectivity to work. As socialist realism sang the praise of industrial work, Reality television shows us how social interaction can produce valuable content as it is put in a particular setting and empowered in a particular direction.

Ubiquitous branding: the mobile internet

The death of distance in telephony means that a call from Rome to New York will cost about the same as a call across town. In the new paradigm, the revenue model is not about phone calls. It is about providing life services to our customers: whatever they want, whenever and however they want it – everything from waking them up in the morning, monitoring their health, and controlling their diary, to providing them with entertainment, locating their children, and keeping watch over them while they sleep.

(Kenny Hirschhorn, Executive Vice President of Strategy, Imagineering and Futurology, Orange[6])

While internet usage has grown rapidly during the 1990s, industry strategists predict that the provision of a functioning mobile internet will alter the nature and sociological function of the medium. Much like the transistor changed the nature of radio listening, it is thought that the 'wired' mobile phone will make internet access ubiquitous and enable the space and time of the internet to effectively merge with the space and time of the everyday. The integration of mobile phones with the internet will thus lead towards a future marked by more or less ubiquitous computing, where information and communication technologies have been effectively integrated into the very environment of social existence. This development has been embraced by industry interests. As the quote above indicates, moving beyond the simple phone call is considered vital for future revenues, or even survival. One important reason for this has to do with the particular economics of the industry.

Since licences for third generation (3G) networks (that provide quicker, continuous internet access) were distributed through public auctions, most telecommunications companies find themselves heavily indebted. Acquiring 3G licences was necessary for company survival, but at the time nobody really knew what to do with them, where future revenues would come from or even if there was going to be sufficient revenue from new services to pay for the substantial investments incurred. Indeed in 2000 an Arthur Anderson report estimated that it would take 15 years for present operators to recuperate their 3G investments (Lindgren *et al.*, 2002). At the same time, the business suffers from over-establishment. And competition is expected to increase with deregulation and new technologies (like Wireless internet) that provide alternatives to the mobile phone as a platform for mobile computing and communications. In this situation continuous growth is crucial to the survival of companies, and most established players aim primarily at increasing their market share (Balsinde *et al.*, 2000). Incumbents do the same. Financially adventurous Hutchinson has pushed the expansion of 3, its new 3G telephone company operating on the European market, by slashing users' fees, and heavy subsidies for phones. At the same time, however, companies know that in the long run the supply of new subscribers is limited, and over time, competition will push call charges downwards. Together with high growth expectations from shareholders this has driven an expansion in services that manage both to tie existing users tighter to the company (reducing 'churn', to use the industry term), and to valorize new areas of their everyday life. The general belief is also that most future revenue will come from such 'premium services'. One

Orange market survey indicates that users are willing to spend up to three times more for such services than for person-to-person communication (Haig, 2002: 40). Indeed, many now speak of Customer Lifetime Management, a strategy that aims at maximizing the overall life-time revenue of customers through a diversified range of services that both tie the customer closer to the company and make its services penetrate deeper into his or her life (Benni *et al.*, 2003; Braff *et al.*, 2003).

These factors have contributed to increasing the importance of branding. On the one hand, branding serves to create stickiness. Here the customer's solidarity with a particular branded provider is important. Traditionally, such solidarities have been encouraged around particular brands of mobile phones that can function as symbolic tokens to signify identity and life-style. Both Nokia and Motorola have invested heavily in building an attractive sign-value around their handsets through design, advertising and product placements. (Motorola supplies communication gear at US sporting events, and figures in the latest James Bond flick, taking the place of Erikson; Nokia does co-promotions with Pepsi-Cola and has had placements in Hollywood successes such as *Minority Report*.) Recently providers have begun to counter, by placing their logo on the phones they provide or, like Orange, launching phones under their own brand. (The Orange SPV – Sound Pictures Video – Smartphone, is powered by Microsoft software and produced and developed by the relatively anonymous hardware manufacturer High Tech Corporation.)

This is part of a general move to enhance the brand value of providers and to encourage customers to see the provider as more than just a supplier of technical services. As one marketing director I interviewed stressed, it is now important to create emotionally significant relations with consumers that enable them to experience the provider as a partner in their daily lives. In part this can be achieved by constructing a coherent brand identity and by investing in advertising, design, cross-promotions and other forms of positioning. Of greater importance, however, is to provide services that contribute to and enhance consumer's everyday existence. In the case of mobile phones, branding means first of all, the inclusion of customer's everyday life within the branded context supplied by the provider: to create a range of services that can function as natural components to customer's everyday life. As the source of revenue thus shifts from network and call charges to the provision of services and 'content', the brand also comes to function for investors as a direct indicator of potential future Customer Lifetime Value. For example, in 1999, Deutche Telecom acquired One2One for £6.9 billion, or £2,460 per customer. Two months later Orange went to Mannesmann for

£5,400 per customer. With similar networks, customer base and operational capacities the price differential was attributed to the stronger brand image of Orange which stood for a 'potential for greater customer lifetime value' (Hamilton and Kirby, 2002).

A second rationale behind this drive towards a real subsumption of users' social lives rests with the social nature of the medium. Mobile phones have developed into a kind of McLuhanesque 'extension' that enables participation in social networks that have developed as a kind of second layer to ordinary life. For one thing, mobile phones allow for a more efficient organization of time, 'they make time denser' (Jauréguiberry, 2000: 256). They work as a kind of 'Lazarus devices' that resurrect socially 'dead time' – on the bus, on the train, waiting in line (cf. Green, 2002; Katz and Aakhus, 2002: 2, ff.; Perry *et al.*, 2001). A growing body of research shows how this freed time is then put to work in the production of social and emotional relations. Teenagers, it seems are particularly apt in using mobile phones for the 'hyper co-ordination' of a fluid and flexible sociality (Ling and Ytri, 2002). Finnish teenagers organize their social life around the cell phone, and particularly around SMS-messaging in a kind of 'SMS nomadism' (Townsend, 2002: 71), floating 'like schools of fish' (Silberman, 1999) between different venues and activities in the city. (The emergence of SMS messaging, originally thought of as a marginal auxiliary service, was largely driven by cash-poor teenagers' attempts to circumvent the billing policies of providers; Haig, 2002: 11.) For them mobile communications have become integral to everyday life (Kasesniemi and Rautiainen, 2002: 170). Similarly, in Tokyo, the mobile phone has become a core component of young people's social life where *oyayubisoku*, 'thumb-tribes' rely on SMS messaging to co-ordinate events and actions (Rheingold, 2003: 4, ff.). Research on Norwegian teenagers shows very similar results. There, the phone, and in particular SMS is employed to 'micro co-ordinate everyday life' but also to achieve a kind of continuous emotional and social connectedness. A large part of the SMS messages exchanged lack any clear purpose. It is often a matter of informing on one's whereabouts, exchanging greetings, chain letters, jokes or different kinds of images. One simply announces one's presence, and one's readiness to connect and participate (Ling and Ytri, 2002). Symptomatically, a 'Japanese schoolgirl' cited by *The Economist* (1999: 5) referred to the mobile as 'an extension of myself'. (And, the Finnish term for mobile phone – *kanny* – means 'extension of the hand'.) The 'Lazarus time' resurrected by the mobile is put to work in producing a kind of sociality that centres on informational networks rather than on physically anchored communities, and that is over-layered on, and made to interact with the (relatively) fixed social interaction systems of the offline world. Mobile phones enable a kind of doubling of the social world, they add on an 'absent presence' that multiplies the possibilities to connect and communicate. This new layer of sociality remains both 'increasingly de-centralized and much more co-ordinated than before' (Lochlannn 2002; Townsend, 2002: 66). For teenagers, for professionals and, increasingly, for people in general, mobiles are a significant component in the production of that mobility (Urry, 2000) or 'network sociality' (Wittel, 2001) which is an important characteristic of, as well as a crucial resource for, post-modern social formations. This new 'putting to work' of time that has been freed up seems to be particularly visible in some places. In Finland, Puro (2002) argues, the contrast is evident between a 'mobile information society that idealizes communication anytime and anyplace' and an existing speech culture that values silence. Mobile phones visibly incite Finns to talk and employ their newfound loquacity in the production of a ubiquitous mobile connectivity.

When integrated into everyday life, mobile phones have become a productive force employed to allow new and highly efficient ways of producing immaterial goods like sociality, events and shared meanings. Concomitantly, the task of mobile branding is evolving to become that of putting this productive power to work in the generation of brand value; shaping the common that consumers/users produce so that it is articu-lated within the branded technological context. The first developments along these lines have been to construct various forms of branded communities. To deliver the promise of its brand Orange launched 'My Orange', a service accessible for Orange subscribers through WAP enabled phones (or just over the internet). My Orange offers a wide range of services, like downloadable calling tunes, games, images (mostly of the innocent kind, but *Playboy* has begun to collaborate with the US provider Legend, and porn on the mobile is one possible future application of MMS technology), graphics, online account servicing and life-style information, like horoscopes, travel information, jokes and drink recipes. So far, the purpose is primarily to strengthen the brand and to develop the technology. Until now, downloadable ring tunes and logos have been the services in most frequent demand, with pictures coming up strongly as MMS enabled phones spread (Poropuras, 2002a; van Impe, 2003). However, predictions are that the fields of expansion are community services, life-style information, gaming and dating. Many providers have experimented with branded communities. Orange has developed a prototype in its 'world community', Orange users all across the world can access information on 'community events' world-wide, consult travel guides and information on life-styles and customs (complete with a phrasebook). They can also interact sending messages and playing games. So far the service is only accessible over the internet (and it does not seem to generate much traffic). The New York based Upoc (universal point of contact) has had much more success in this respect. The service maintains many different communities, like 'nyc terrorism alert' or 'prayer of the day' where members can circulate information via SMS. The most popular is the 'celebrity watch' community where members inform each other on the whereabouts of celebrities. Apart from the thrill of physically present movie stars, the service, like *Epinions*, thrives on its ability to put community and peer recognition to work: says Upoc CEO Gordon Gould, 'It's very obvious and apparent to people what the rules are . . . . If I see a celebrity – bang! – I send a message. That's really easy. All of a sudden I'm culturally relevant' (Haig, 2002: 36). This potential experience of being 'culturally relevant', appreciated by one's peers as a source of timely and relevant information provides an attractive add-on to the service that efficiently motivates people to contribute. A similar service that is projected to expand in the future is mobile gaming. Indeed analysts see this as the most important trend in the short run (Poropudas, 2002b), as the enormous success of the recent NokiaGame has shown (the game had to close its doors to further participants after having already attracted over a million players). Traditional game producers like Nintendo come under new threats as mobile producers, like Nokia, merge with game manufacturers and launch their own gaming consoles, like the Nokia N-gage (Poropudas, 2002c). Mobile interactive games can be played out in real space and create a kind of second layer of playful sociality. One case in point is the popular Stockholm bot-fighters game, where (mostly) young men roam the streets armed with mobile phones, trying to kill each other's 'bots', software robots representing the players. Through location based technology, the game is played out in real space (Rheingold, 2003: 18). So far these games are rather primitive, but there are plans to launch successful games like Hitman in a mobile, interactive version, as soon as available bandwidth permits this.

Indeed, as the Japanese i-mode experience has shown, customer participation tends to generally boost the attraction of services. As this example shows, the potential of gaming, as well as most other services will be greatly enhanced by 3G technology. This is because 3G will allow a faster continuous internet connection, higher bandwith (which permits streaming images and video) and, most importantly, the ability to track the physical location of users. This allows physical presence to become a variable in the formation of interactive contexts and the sharing of information. Location based information also adds value to chat and dating services. These have become popular even with 2G telephones, that do not allow for location-specific information. Vodaphone has launched a chat service as well as an anonymous SMS flirtation service where users can exchange messages with another Vodaphone subscriber of their chosen gender and sexual orientation. However, location makes the service 'more real'. Like the Japanese Lovegetty (a device that rings if a compatible partner is within a specified distance), the addition of location simplifies the passage from mediated sociality to face-to-face encounters. Match.com had this in mind while initiating co-operation with AT&T mobile in the United Stats. Using location-based technologies the service will alert users to the presence of potential partners with matching characteristics in their vicinity. Through a co-branding programme, daters are then pointed to the nearest Starbucks for a safe and relaxed first date. These sort of co-branding efforts also seem to be the future of mobile marketing. There is a widespread consensus that advertising on the mobile phone will not work as in the case of older broadcasting media. People do not want to receive streams of commercial SMS or MMS messages. Rather, it is important to make commercial messages an integrated part of the services through which users structure their lives. Users should, ideally not be able to distinguish between 'information' and 'advertising'. One successful example is the Magazine *Men's Health* and its 'Belly off Club' where the magazine provides daily calorie conscious menus via SMS to readers who have registered for the service. Another is *Cosmopolitan*'s SMS alerts about ways to improve sex life (it is suggested that these messages be passed on to boyfriends by *Cosmopolitan*'s primarily heterosexual female audience, thus generating additional traffic). Similarly, Bridget Jones's Mobile offered a series of daily text messages from Bridget to launch the film. Both these campaigns were successfully aimed at paying customers, and some form of user consent is generally regarded as a condition for using the mobile as a vehicle for advertising. One way of achieving this is to have an advertiser supply a free service that is attractive in its own right. For example, Vodaphone has launched a restaurant guide that uses location information to point at the nearest bar, restaurant or club. The service also chooses a venue for the occasion, 'Whether you're taking your boss out for lunch, going for a romantic meal, or just fancy a takeaway, we've got the place for you'. In the future, this service could conceivably be provided by *Guide Michelin* or some other branded guide. Similar initiatives are already underway. Orange co-brands with Mastercard to handle payments for upcoming E-commerce services. Vodaphone co-brands with Manchester United to provide football information and gossip. Probably co-branding will be even more frequent as the range of content on offer increases.

Co-branding can be a strategy to guarantee quality content. Services like these aim at making the brand Vodaphone 'an even more important part of our customers' lives'. Or, which is the same thing, to make an increasing range of activities within that life evolve within a branded context. Mobile internet thus promises to take branding one step further, producing a kind of ubiquitous branded space, in which significant parts of users' lives transpire. As it unfolds in an increasingly mediatized life-world, everyday social interaction is always already anticipated to produce particular forms of valuable content, or to contribute to the accumulation of lived meanings and experiences that make up the basis of brand equity.

Reality and automation

> If one takes a long-term historical perspective there are compelling reasons for seeing the mobile marketplace as the next step of a developmental process that has been underway for many hundreds of years – and that will finally culminate in individualization, the immediate satisfaction of needs and a longing for freedom.
>
> (Lindgren *et al.*, 2002: 3)

Perhaps it is the (Swedish) author's scant familiarity with the English language, perhaps it is an unintended slip on the part of this basically optimistic and celebratory management consultant, but the combination of an 'immediate satisfaction of needs' and a continuous 'longing for freedom' seems indeed to be a feasible future scenario. As the previous chapter proposed and this chapter has developed, brand management techniques can be located according to the degrees of intensity and universality that they permit. On the one hand we have initiatives that permit an intensive control of user activity within a restricted space, like the branded commercial environment or the highly managed community. On the other hand we have strategies that aim at a high degree of universality, but where user activity is difficult to steer, like the combined initiatives that have given a ubiquitous presence to brands like Coca-Cola. Usually, these are combined with some form of surveillance of user activity that creates feedback into the brand elaboration process. In the New Media environment the same distinctions apply. On the one hand we have initiatives like dating sites and MMOPRGs where user interaction is heavily guided. On the other hand we have plans for a coming ubiquitous branding of everyday life through the spread of the mobile internet. In both of these instances principles developed offline are taken one step further. The MMOPRG produces a particular Reality that effectively constitutes parts of the subjectivity of the actor. The mediatization of everyday life through mobile internet creates a feedback that not only contributes to the development of brand image, but that actually works towards the automation of life itself. Ubiquitous computing – the presence of processors able to communicate in household appliances, clothes and money – points towards the possibility of a flexible reality that bends and adapts to the individual user's particular preferences. We already have highway billboards changing as they tune into the radio stations listened to by passing cars. Many similar examples of personalization of reality might come in the near future. Present industry research is investigating the potentiality of ubiquitous computing, 'beyond 3G' to personalize reality and to make life more productive. Not only in terms of work, but also in terms of personal gratification of 'life-style': proactive healthcare, 'Family Management' and 'Life Management'; political engagement: eCitizenship, eGovernment and the use of communication technology for local direct democracy; consumer choices, many of which will be automated by ambient intelligence, like the self-restocking refrigerator. The political and existential implications of this are potentially enormous and would require substantial research in their own right. I will not attempt anything in that direction here. Let me instead comment on its possible implications for an emerging political economy of life. Since most, if not all, of these new forms of customized Reality will be commercial, it is likely that the mediatization of life will also entail its complete commercialization, its total subsumption under capital. This will probably entail two things. First, ubiquitous computing is likely to mean ubiquitous surveillance as the extraction of information about preferences and life-styles will be crucial to the provision of viable commercial services. We have already seen this development on the internet where a well nigh ever-present 'panoptic sort' (Gandy, 1993) transforms most of our activities online into commodified information. As our cars, refrigerators and clothes begin to gather information about us, our everyday world will probably fill up with many more such 'surveillant assemblages' (Haggerty and Ericson, 2000). This way the very contingency of life itself is effectively put to work as a form of labour that generates what will become an increasingly valuable commodity, information that can be transformed into content, in some form. But, this information will generally be used to produce services that aim at the automation of life. The customized reality is nothing but a way of automatically selecting away everything that might not be of interest to us, to automatically generate order out of the complexity of living. Life in a tailored reality will come to resemble the life of video game characters like Lara Croft, for whom Pole (2000) has brilliantly observed,

> everything is fanatically, obsessively 'true' in three dimensions. There is no room for interesting fuzziness or spatial ambiguity . . .. The whole Tomb Raider world is utterly dependent on Lara's size and animations. The distance she can jump, reach, run forward and fall are set variables. In this way, her world is designed for her to exist in.
> (Pole, 2000: 232–4)

In such a smooth space surprises are, so to say, ruled out a priori by automation. My refrigerator, my radio, my car and computer automatically select what I want without me having to put in any effort. While this might be of great convenience in many instances, the main problem for capital is that the more life becomes automated, the less value it can produce. The whole purpose behind branding has been to put the creative power of life to work in the generation of immaterial values. That creative power is mainly manifest in the use of consumer goods. But if that aspect of life too becomes automated, branding, as a paradigm of valorization will eventually run into a deep contradiction. If every freedom is situated, anticipated and partially automated, then a 'longing for (a less predetermined kind of) freedom' might indeed be a general subjective wish. But it will also become a systemic requirement since only such not entirely predictable freedoms can generate the ethical surplus necessary for the extraction of value from the social.

6 The brand as informational capital

In her rich and insightful book, *Brands: The Logos of the Global Economy*, Celia Lury argues that the brand, in its contemporary format could be understood as a 'new media object'. Emerging at the 'intersection of the diverse histories of computing, information technology and media as well as those of economics, marketing and design' the brand embodies the logic of the new media, as described by Manovich (Lury, 2004: 6; Manovich, 2001). First, she argues, brands are dynamic, multi-layered and open ended, this way they embody the incompleteness and variability that characterizes new media objects. Second, the brand works as an interface between producers and consumers; this way it promotes forms of interactivity, typical of new media in general. This, Lury argues, also makes the brand a good example both of the (general) 'status of the object' in the information age, and (to follow her pun) the 'object-ive' that contemporary capitalism tends to pursue: an open ended, interactive relation to the consumer (ibid.: 151). In this concluding chapter I would like to expand on Lury's suggestion to argue that brands can be understood to exemplify, not only the status of objects in the information age, but also the very logic of informational capital. (Indeed, drawing on Lukács [1971], one could argue that it is its being a sort of paradigmatic manifestation of the logic of capital that also makes the brand into what Lury argues is an ontological paradigm.) Like the factory in times of Fordism, the brand stands out as a central institutionalization, a concrete manifestation of the abstract logic of accumulation that drives capital in the information age. What then is capital; what is its logic; what is the logic of informational capital, and how does the brand embody it?

Capital is a complex object. From one point of view, capital is a thing. It is a tool that is employed to produce something, a means of production. A hammer, a steamroller, or a computer can work as capital in relation to the labour of some living human subject that employs it. From another point of view, capital embodies a relation of power. The machine, the factory, the computer contain a series of affordances and constraints that pushes the labour process to evolve in a particular way, in accordance with the functional requirements of the particular production process. From a third point of view, capital is an embodiment of value. Different assets, factories, machinery, goodwill appear on balance sheets as resources that can be capitalized on, that can work as collaterals for loans or support the price of stock. From this point of view, 'capital' is a temporary fixation, a reification of the production process, it is 'dead labour' to use a Marxist definition. Capital can thus be understood as three different things: a means of production, a form of governance, and a form of value. What then is the logic of capital? It is the abstract totality that unites these three aspects. The logic of capital can be defined as a description of the particular dynamics of capital as value-in-progress (Bellofiore, 1998). It describes the ways in which value passes from a fluid state (in the form of money) into a fixed state through investments in machinery, factories, media presence and other means of production; the ways in which these means of production govern and control the labour process and how the surplus value thus produced is again translated into monetizeable forms of value. (Marx described this process with his famous M-C-M' – Money-Capital-MoreMoney-formula.) When the concept of a 'logic of capital' was popular in the late 1970s and early 1980s, the assumption was often that there was *one* logic of capital, modelled on industrial capitalism, and that the form of its particular dynamics, rationalization and standardization would eventually spread to all sectors of society. I think it is better to assume that there can be different logics that correspond to different forms of capital, and that these can co-exist to different degrees. That way it becomes possible to think of the logic of informational capital as distinct from that of industrial capital. How then does this logic look, and how is it embodied by the brand? I will discuss these questions under the three headings below: *immateriality*, *programming* and *value*.

Immateriality

As a means of production, informational capital is immaterial capital. Things like web-portals, knowledge capital and social capital have use-values that reside, not in their concrete manifestations (pixels on a screen, databases, and so on), as much as in the social or symbolic relations that they can mobilize. The social capital of a firm is useful insofar as the network of relations that it encompasses enables me to do certain things. Brands too are useful in their immateriality. Branded objects are but partial manifestations of the 'essence' or 'personality' of the brand. This is something that moves on the abstract levels of 'emotion', 'experience' or 'metaphysics', too abstract sometimes to be put into words (Feldwick, 1999). This essence, dear to the more metaphysical line of managerial literature, is but a mystification of the relational nexus that the brand embodies. And it is this relational network that makes up the core of its productive utility as an everyday tool. When I use a brand, the network of meaningful social and aesthetic relations that has been established around it enables me to perform a certain personality or relate to a certain group of people. What brand-owners own is the privilege of guarding and deriving value from this relational network, and, as Chapter 1 referred, it is the extension of the relational nexus that the brand contains that is guarded by contemporary trademark law. However, brands do not only consist in relations between things, but in relations between things, people, images, texts and physical and informational environments. This way brands embody the cross-mediality that marks informational capital in general. (As in the case of 'content brands', like *Lord of the Rings* that move between different media platforms, or knowledge capital that links texts, databases and individual brains.) Brands are a perfect example of the integration of 'aesthetic production . . . into commodity production generally' that early theorists of 'The Post-Modern' noted long ago (cf. Jameson, 1991).

This relational nature of brands also means that they are not located to any particular physical place. A bit like divinities they are everywhere and nowhere. (A brandspace, like Niketown, might work as a kind of temple, but the usefulness of the Nike brand is by no means located to that particular place, but can be invoked in many walks of life.) To this 'placelessness' of the brand corresponds a general de-territorialization of the informational production process. Production can no longer be confined to the factory, through mediatization the extended, immaterial production process has come to invest the social as a whole. Labour, Antonio Negri writes, has been socialized to the point of becoming 'coextensive with reproduction' to coincide with life itself (Negri, 1999: 83). The brand thus corresponds to the condition of a 'network culture' where the mediatization of the social has progressed to the point that it is no longer meaningful to maintain a distinction between media and reality, where information is no longer something that represents reality, but something that provides an ambience in which reality can unfold. Like media in the information age, capital is not something that one confronts in a particular place (the factory), as much as it is something 'within which' one lives one's everyday life. The brand is one example of capital as an informational milieu. Brands are inserted into the environment of life where they work as a sort of 'platform for action' (Lury, 2004: 6).

Finally, like knowledge capital, web-portals or computer programs, brands are dynamic, open ended and constantly upgradeable. (This goes for industrial machinery too, but there the upgrading process is slower and more difficult.) Brand managers deploy a number of feedback loops to learn from their users. Brand management is about keeping in touch with, and if possible anticipate an evolving socialized production process. Indeed, it can be argued that such anticipation, or 'programming' is the particular form of governance that the brand deploys.

Programming

Brands are like computer programs, Lury argues. Like a computer program the brand consists of information deployed to produce information. Brands are complexes of information that enter into the informational flows of daily life and direct and anticipate it in particular ways. As Chapter 5 has shown, brand management is about anticipating possible ways of feeling with and relating to the brand. In this respect, brands are made by a kind of loop, similar to those employed in computer programming (*if* you choose this brand of coffee, *then* this kind of experience becomes possible . . .). It is important to notice that these loops are not binding. Other forms of experiences, uses and attitudes are possible. There are seldom sanctions. As a form of governance, programming is not restrictive as much as it is enabling. Brands, like many other forms of contemporary governance, rule through the freedom of its subjects, empowering them in particular directions (Barry, 2001; Dean, 1999; Rose, 1999). Sometimes such empowering loops can be merely symbolic; at other times they have more tangible manifestations (architecture that directs the flow of impressions in a branded space, websites that link to other websites, branded computer operating systems, like the Apple Mac OS X that automatically contains particular forms of software, like iTunes, which in turn link to particular commercial ventures: the iTunes music store). The genealogy of programming can be traced back to what Michel Foucault called 'governmentality' (or 'government') – what he identified as the third principle of modern power (along with 'discipline' and 'sovereignty'). While both sovereignty and discipline are restrictive forms of power (with the difference that in the case of sovereignty the force of the law is external and in the case of discipline it is internal, it works through education and internalization), government is not. It is enabling, it is about making it possible for a series of diverse social processes to achieve a 'series of specific finalities':

> With government it is a question, not of imposing law on men, but on disposing things: that is to say, of employing tactics rather than laws, and even of using laws themselves as tactics – to arrange things in such a way that, through a certain number of means, such and such ends may be achieved.
>
> (Foucault, 1991: 95)

Foucault linked government to a specific modern discipline – economics – and its emergence to the discovery of the problem of 'population'. This object of government, population-economy, in turn materialized through a particular technology: statistics. Now, the development of statistics, as Manovich shows, has been closely tied to the deployment of information processing devices: from the simple manual tabulations of Quesnay, through the mechanical calculators, tabulating machines and punch card computers (such as the IBM machines used in Nazi Germany to keep track of the Jewish population; cf. Black, 2001), up to the computers that revolutionized the processing of statistics from the late 1960s and on, and made complex operations such as clustering, profiling and data-mining possible. This close connection between government on the one hand, and information processing technology on the other makes it possible to suggest that government, governing 'from below' through tactics of enabling, empowering and programming, can be considered a logic of power particular to informational capital. In the way that discipline reached its fullest development in the factory system (and the other institutions, like schools and prisons that mimicked that model), where spatial and temporal re-composition, together with the omnipresent, objective rule of the machine made possible new and more radical forms of re-education and reform, government, although originally developed much earlier, reaches its fullest development with the ubiquitous spread of information technology. First, because electronic media, and in particular information and communications media, enhance the autonomous productivity of the social. These media enable the social to evolve within an informational environment where a commonly available means of production, a General Intellect, is freely available, inscribed in the environment itself, and can be drawn upon in a wide variety of autonomous and more or less spontaneous practices. They also allow the emergence of a sort of self-organizing, micro-coordinating network sociality (Castells, 1996). Information technologies and the media milieus they help to foster give a productive autonomy to everyday life that in a sense renders discipline superfluous. Second, because information and communications systems allow a ubiquitous surveillance of this autonomous productivity. Data mining, life-style clustering, cookies and other online tracking devices, information systems that link cash registers, bar codes and information gathered through loyalty cards create a myriad of feedback points through which the autonomous productivity of the social can contribute to, alter and refine programming strategies. (One of the simplest, and most ingenious of such feedback systems was perhaps the *Kai-ban* system employed in Japanese factories in the early 1970s: pieces of paper flowing 'downstream' in the production chain allowed for a real time adjustment of the production process throughout the factory; Marazzi, 1999b.) Third, because information and communications media allow a decomposition of social processes into variables relevant to the particular process that one tries to program. As they move through the surveyed informational environment, individuals dissolve into data-clouds: life-style preferences indicated, particular web-surfing itineraries, purchasing patterns, and so on. These can later be recomposed into data sets like life-style or customer profile that can feed directly into particular programming strategies. Information technologies thus allow the object of government to shift over from the individual to the social and, in turn, the over-layering of the social with a surveying assemblage that provides continuous feedback in the form of relevant kinds of data sets. The autonomous productivity of the social, of the networked multitude can thus be immediately re-coded into the relevant kinds of information. This enables a superior solution to what Tiziana Terranova (2004: 122) identifies as the over-riding problem of governance under informational capitalism: 'to steer the spontaneous activities [of the productive multitude] to plateaus that are desirable and preferable'. The response is 'the definition of a new biopolitical plane that can be organized through the deployment of an immanent control, which operates directly within the productive power of the multitude'. Brands exercise a sort of management governance.

Brand management embodies this logic of ubiquitous surveillance and programming. The productivity of consumers unfolds in an informational environment where the brand acts as a kind of program, a platform for action, a loop that anticipates choices of actions. At the same time consumer practice unfolds under more or less constant surveillance, where its autonomous productivity is translated into relevant forms of feedback. Brand management operates in a kind of social factory where the informational environment (of which the brand itself is a part) functions both as a commonly available means of production and a ubiquitous means of surveillance and governance.

This state of things is linked to the particular problem that informational capital faces: the successful appropriation of externalities. Unlike industrial capitalism, where most of the production process took place in the factory, under the direct control of capital, the production process today unfolds to a large extent beyond the direct control of capital. Much of the value of brands derives from the free (in the sense of both unpaid and autonomous) productivity of consumers; the same thing goes for web-portals and knowledge intensive service companies. In these instances, labour is in effect 'in a non-place in respect to capital' (Negri, 1999: 82) beyond its direct command, and the extraction of surplus value entails some form of appropriation of the fruits of that autonomous productivity, of valuable externalities. Brand management solves this problem by positioning the brand as a kind of virtual factory, by giving labour a place where its autonomous productivity more or less directly translates into feedback and information. But this is not enough. Brand management must also ensure that what the multitude produces emerges as a quality that is compatible with other qualities, that this productivity unfolds on a 'platform that is desirable and preferable'. This is the purpose of programming. Brands evolve with the activity of the social, but in programmed ways, so that the qualities that they represent stay compatible. Brand management is thus about a reflexive filtering of the productivity of the multitude and its re-insertion into the social as a polished quality. Incompatible expressions of that productivity, expressions that makes reality enter unfiltered, like people who want to have the word 'sweatshop' on their Nike sneakers, are censored. Indeed, the anti-branding activists, who have understood that the value of brands resides precisely in their existence as *compatible* qualities, concentrate their attacks at penetrating these 'reality filters' and introducing elements of incompatibility.

Value

Brands move with the evolution of qualities on the part of a productive multitude, and translate these into a plane of compatibility. Like money, brands thus work as a kind of generalized medium of communication, a sort of currency. But, in contrast to money, this currency does not reduce quality to quantity but ensures the global communicability and compatibility of a particular quality (Lury, 2004; Luhmann, 1995). (And one could argue that this capitalist objective of making qualities compatible began with the TQM – Total Quality Management – movement in the 1980s.) This way, brands also embody what Manovich lists as a prominent quality of new media: modularity. Like the compatibility of software units that capture different forms of content (education, children's cartoons, sex, violence, and so on) branded qualities – Shell petrol in the gas-guzzling Hummer on your way to buy Fair Trade groceries – can be assembled without any of the individual qualities being affected in themselves. It is this communicability and compatibility of the brand that makes up the source of its use-value, both for consumers and for corporations. For the consumer the brand is useful as long as it can enter into an assemblage where it, together with other brands, achieves something (an expression, a relation, an emotion). For corporations it is the autonomous or creative brand assemblage that consumers engage in that generates the valuable feedback that keeps the brand evolving. It is this assemblage that is monitored by means of techniques like coolhunting, customer profiling, data mining and so on, and programmed through the management and establishment of relations through product placements, cross-branding and such. By making qualities compatible brands thus embody the general form of value of informational capital, its communicability, its ability to be shared, networked, compiled and transferred (Negri, 1996: 151; Lash, 2002).

This communicability is also the substance of the monetary value of the brand. It is this aspect that is paid for on the two principle markets where brand values are realized. On a first and most basic level, consumers pay for access to the brand. Within the marketing and accounting literature this is usually conceived of as the 'premium price' that consumers pay for a branded item, with respect to a 'comparable' non-branded item (a Nike shoe versus an anonymous shoe, for example). What consumers pay for is access to the communicative potential of the brand, the possibility of inserting the brand in their own assemblage of compatible qualities. The use-value of the brand for the consumer is its value as a means of communicative production. The premium price pays for access, not ownership. This is directly evident in the increasingly frequent leasing or rental schemes that, for example, car companies engage in. Here consumers pay for a multidimensional long-term relationship with the brand over and beyond the functionality or life time of individual products (like cars; Lury, 2004; Rifkin, 2000). But the principle is the same when consumer goods are actually purchased. Here the object, the good, works as a sort of medium of access to the brand. Most brands supply a plurality of such access media. If I can't afford a pair of Nike sneakers, perhaps I can afford a cap or a T-shirt. If I can't afford a Mercedes car, perhaps I can afford a bike. The car will always be better than the bike, but the bike will also be worth a premium price insofar as it too gives access to the brand as a communicative tool, and allows me to produce certain things.

Brand values also illustrate a second central principle of informational capitalism, the separation of production and valorization. In industrial capitalism, the most important point of realization of values was the consumer market, and, as Keynesianism suggested this mechanism depended in the end on the purchasing power of the very people that produced the objects to be sold. Production and valorization were close, connected through the factory and its vertically integrated distribution system. A key tendency in the development away from Fordism has been the growing importance of financial markets. But values on financial markets are only tenuously linked to material production. Often, what is valorized on financial markets is more linked to the risks and insecurities of life itself. This is particularly visible in strategies like the privatization of housing, pensions and social insurance systems, which have established a direct link between everyday life and financial capital. These instances illustrate a more general principle of the 'financialization of bio-political risks' (Marazzi, 1999a). As 'production' has tended to become 'coextensive with reproduction' and coincide with life itself (Negri, 1999: 83), value has been abstracted into a complicated estimate of reproductive risks and possibilities. On financial markets brand values too, represent a sort of financialization of bio-political risks. True it is not so much a matter of the tangible risks of illness, old age and unemployment that fuel financial values through pension funds and insurance companies. Rather it is a matter of the inherently risky nature or, perhaps better, instability of identity. For consumers brands are a way of producing the self and the social connectedness that provides it with moorings in an inherently unstable social environment, where things like identity and community are no longer given by tradition or social structure in any straightforward way. The consumer is posited as a kind of entrepreneurial self that 'itself' bears the responsibility for the elaboration of his or her 'human capital'; his or her sanity, mobility, aptitude to variable hours and circumstances of work, cultural capital and the general 'up-to-date-ness' of his or her knowledge, both instrumental, aesthetic and symbolic (Gorz, 2003: 5; du Gay, 1996). In the form of this entrepreneurial self-management each person is responsible for the production of her own self as an economically valuable resource. Financial brand values build on estimates of the productive potential of the brand within this process of communicative construction of stability in a fluid world. (And this fundamental instability and amorality of the social is also at the heart of popular contemporary narratives of 'memes', 'selfish genes' or the influential 'tipping point' theory of Malcolm Gladwell, 2002; cf. Terranova, 2004.)

In the marketing and accounting literature, the substance of brand values is generally referred to as *brand equity*. Brand equity stands for the resources that the brand can mobilize: 'a set of brand assets and liabilities linked to a brand its name and symbol that add to or subtract from the value provided by a product or service to a firm and/or to that firm's customers' (Aaker, 1991: 15; Aaker's book *Managing Brand Equity* is an early classic, the first to give a substantive academic treatment of the problem of brand management). Aaker defines brand equity along five dimensions (and that definition persists with some variations): (1) Brand Loyalty: the existence of a more or less loyal customer base. (2) Name Awareness: the extent to which consumers in general are familiar to the brand. (3) Perceived Quality: the perception of the overall quality of the brand which is 'not necessarily based on a knowledge of detailed specification' (Aaker, 1991: 19) – the idea that people have of the brand, for short. (4) Brand Associations: the attitudes or feelings that a brand generates, and (5) 'Other proprietary Brand Assets', such as patents, trademarks and channel relationships. An important dimension here is the control of the concrete distribution chain (access to shelf space and so on) that a brand-owning company can exercise. For our purposes, we can define brand equity as the productive power of the social and symbolic relations that have evolved around the brand, their ability to *add to or subtract from the value provided by a product or a service.* Recently it has been recognized that the most important aspect of brand equity is the actual standing that the brand has in the lived reality of consumers: what is known as 'Customer-based Brand Equity', which Keller defines as 'the knowledge that has been created around the brand in consumers' minds' (1993: 1). It is this 'share of mind', the presence of the brand as a potential 'platform for action' which is supposed to underpin financial realizations of brand value. As with, for example, web-portals, brand equity represents a kind of 'virtual real estate' (Schiller, 1999). It stands for the potential attention that can be accumulated through the programmed relationality that makes up the brand.

But brand values illustrate another central principle of informational capitalism: the fundamental immeasurability of values. Brand values build on qualities like attention, association, loyalty and emotional or other subjective investments, that lend themselves to measurement only with great difficulty. There are of course ways around this problem, like the various forms of residual measurement that simply equate brand value with the market price of a company minus its tangible (measurable) assets. But most widely used measurement methods, like the Interbrand method (that is used to compile *Business Week*'s yearly list of the *World's Most Valuable Brands*) build on some estimate of the value of these immeasurable qualities. Usually, this is done through the use of some sort of more or less arbitrary indicators. For example, the Interbrand method builds on a combination of estimations of future cash flows attributable to the brand, and a multiplier that estimates the attention based strength and leverage of the brand itself (Murphy, 2001). The first, financial measurement is based on a calculation of the difference between operational revenue actually generated during the last three to five years and an appreciation of what a similar but unbranded product would have generated. While this is in itself a problematic measurement (how do you find a similar yet unbranded product?) the calculation multiplier is even more dubious. It builds on an estimate and subsequent ranking of seven different dimension of brand strength. They are: leadership (essentially market share), stability (the position that the brand occupies in the cultural universe of consumers), reference market (the make up of the brand's market), the stability of the market itself, internationality (the international diffusion of the brand), trend (the actuality of the brand in the culture of consumers), support (marketing investments), and protection (the extent to which the brand can be legally defended). While these measurements might be as fair as any, the problem remains, as one author of a brand valuation textbook underlines, their inherent subjectivity: 'not only in relation to the selection of criteria for the seven different variables, but even more so in the case of their relative weight in constructing the overall multiplier' (Predovic, 2004: 232). Why would these measurements measure the value of the 'standing of a brand in the minds of consumers, better than any others'? And how can you possibly know how much the fact that consumers tend to mention Nivea before Rexona is worth in monetary terms? Brand valuation, like most instruments for the valuation of intellectual capital rely on a set of more or less arbitrarily chosen criteria that are transformed into quantifiable variables in some way. The validity of these measurements is not so much guaranteed by their accuracy, as it is secured by their legitimacy. As long as more or less everybody accepts a method of brand valuation, that method will provide valid results. Indeed, as one CEO of a reputation management firm I talked to expressed, there is a continuous demand for new and more valid measurements that can translate things like attention given to brands, or a corporation's ethical standing into quantitative figures.

One could claim that the difficulties in measuring brand values are linked to the properties of what is measured. It is difficult to measure subjective attachments like attention or affect. This might be true to some extent, but the history of market and audience research shows that capital has had little problem in finding valid ways to measure and valorize these things. The culture industries have for a long time based the valorization of their products upon a measure of the value of viewer attention, mostly in terms of number (and sometimes kinds of) people watching and viewing time. That way the value of a 30 second commercial on prime time could be established as against the value of a 45 second commercial in the afternoon (cf. Ang, 1991; Smythe, 1981). What has vanished is rather the very possibility of using time as a measure. This proposes that the problem of measure that comes to the fore in brand valuation is political, rather than ontological.

To Marxist economics, value is not a substance, but a relation. Two things become valuable if they are put in a relation of exchangeability – united by a common measure, so to say. Now, to valorize; to enable the production of use-values to generate surplus value, means primarily to establish a relation of exchangeability. In this sense, the 'law of value' is not only a term for the prevailing relations of exchange: it is the very foundation for capitalist command of the social. For a long time, the law of value has established labour time as the measure. Things have been exchangeable according to some (mostly very abstract) idea of the amount of abstract labour (time) needed for their production. This measure can be said to have had a 'natural' foundation in nineteenth-century capitalism, to the extent that it could be said to be enforced by the 'invisible hand' of the market. But labour time as a measure becomes problematic already within industrial capitalism. This is because the real subsumption of labour – its inclusion into a factory or even system wide production process – means that labour itself tends to become all the more complex. It relies on and puts to work the social relations and communicative networks – the forms of co-operation – that prevail within the factory environment. This means that the productivity of labour is increasingly derived from things like co-operation, communication and General Intellect that are immanent to the productive environment itself, and do not have their ontological foundation in any external reality that can be invoked as a standard. That way labour time loses its relevance as a measure. As Marx describes the consequences of these developments in the Grundrisse: 'as soon as labour in the direct form has ceased to be the great well-spring of wealth, labour time ceases and must cease to be its measure, and hence exchange value [must cease to be] the measure of use value' (Marx, 1973[1939]: 705). The Fordist project can be understood as a reaction against this 'crisis of value'. The state steps in and guarantees a politically enforced law of value, which establishes the exchangeability between elements *as if* they were measurable in terms of labour time. The assignment of 'values' is arbitrary already here: the labour of male factory workers is given high value, that of female housewives practically no value. But brand management has to face a situation where capital no longer commands the productivity of the social, not even through the state apparatus. The productivity of the networked multitude evolves beyond the command of capital, and therefore also beyond any measure. This way, the instability of measure corresponds to a real separation between production and valorization, and hence a general weakness of capitalist command.

Brands are a capitalist response to the hypermediatization of the social that prevails in informational capitalism. This has not only entailed a fusion of the aesthetic and the economic, of media and reality, of the attention economy and the industrial economy. It has also created the conditions for a real productive autonomy on the part of the inhabitants of this hypermediated world, the networked multitude. Within the forms of immaterial production that the multitude employs (the production of life, of knowledge, of social organization), there is a real possibility for the autonomous production of a common world. It is this surplus that can produce a common that makes up the intrinsic political potential of the multitude: its ability to transcend (or better perhaps 'sidestep') the present and construct a different world, from below (Hardt and Negri, 2004). This is not a utopian prospect. The multitude engages in such practices of 'transformative virtuality' (Terranova, 2004: 20) everyday, in communicative, immaterial production processes, 'a different world' becomes not only possible, but is produced and concretely realized all the time (on the internet, in the self-organizing team, in the slum; cf. Appadurai, 2002). Brand management also feeds off this surplus. It is the possibility of consumers to create something new, their ability to produce what I have called an ethical surplus that is the substance of brand values. The purpose of brand management is to program (or 'hack'; Terranova, 2004) the productive potential of the networked multitude so that it evolves in particular and desirable directions: on the preferred and desirable plane of the brand where all qualities are compatible and the real world is filtered out. It is coherent with this logic of power that the creation of alternative forms of communality are clamped down upon if they are too successful, as in the case of the British 1990s Rave scene, the Italian occupied houses or recent file sharing communities. (Not all of these forms of communality are benign from a western middle class point of view as in the case of right wing or religious – Christian or Muslim – fundamentalism.) This way brand management can be understood as a vanguard form of capitalist (or imperial, to use Hardt and Negri's [2000] term) governance. It recognizes and seeks to benefit from the most advanced forms of negation of the capitalist order: the productive autonomy of the social that is at the same time a political and an economic force. But at the same time, the separation of production from valorization that this entails is a sign of the weakness of capitalist command. There, as in many other instances of immaterial production (sustainable energy solutions, medical research, the provision of basic service for the poor, and so on), capitalist command goes against and acts as an obstacle to the development of the productive forces of the social. The forces of production are becoming too advanced to be contained within capitalist relations of production. The contradiction that the brand embodies, between increased dependency on the productivity of the social and a reduced ability to command that productivity is indicative of a general crisis of informational capitalism.

Notes

1 Introduction

1 Lovemarks is a website (now paired with a book with the same name) set up by the Saatchi & Saatchi advertising agency, and devoted to take brands to 'a future beyond brands'. A lovemark is a brand that 'reaches your heart as well as your mind, creating an intimate, emotional connection that you just can't live without. Ever.' (www.lovemarks.com)

2 Consumption

1 However, in other places Marx stressed the dialectical relation between consumption and production. On the one hand, and quite obviously, production is also consumption, insofar as raw material and machinery are 'consumed' in the process. On the other hand, however, consumption is also production: it is no mere 'end-station' but a process in which the 'product becomes a real product': 'a product becomes a real product only by being consumed. For example, a garment becomes a real garment only in the act of being worn; a house where no one lives is in fact not a real house; thus the product, unlike a mere natural object, proves itself to be, becomes a product only through consumption' (Marx, 1973[1939]: 91). Here then, consumption is a more central concern. Not only is consumption the place where the needs, desires, whims or meanings that gives production a 'motive' are produced, or 'performed'. But, as Miranda (1998) has argued, capital here appears to depend on an extended productive circuit which *includes the meaningful practice of consumption*. It is *through* consumption that a place for capital in the life-world is performed, so to speak. Viewed this way, consumption is no longer outside of 'the social movement' or beyond the scope of political economy, but an integrated element in the capitalist production process, and thus worth including in an analysis of capitalism. This chapter will offer a Marx-inspired perspective on consumption that is influenced by this dialectical view.

2 With this they mean something similar to the ongoing, autonomous 'production of the social' emphasized by many post-modernist scholars (Beck, 1992;

Maffesoli, 1996; Urry, 2000). The common is to be understood 'not as a pre-constituted entity and not as an organic substance that is a by-product of the national community, or *Gemeinschaft*, but rather as the productive activity of singularities in the multitude' (Hardt and Negri, 2004: 206).

3 To capital, living labour, or human life in itself, has no value. Only when life has been organized into labour power can it potentially create value. Capitalist expansion thus proceeds through the 'inclusion' of human life and its transformation into productive labour power. Marx calls this the 'subsumption of labour under capital'. Marx distinguishes between 'formal' and 'real' subsumption. In the case of 'formal subsumption' capitalism 'takes over' an existing labour process which has 'developed before the emergence of a specifically capitalist mode of production' (or, in any case with a certain autonomy in relation to capital). In this case, the wage-relation replaces feudal hierarchies, slave ownership or other non- or pre-capitalist relations of production, *but the labour process in itself does not change much*. A case in point would be 'a peasant who has always produced enough for his needs [who] becomes a day labourer working for a farmer' (Marx, 1990 [1867]: 1020). This stands 'in striking contrast' to the central characteristic of the 'specifically capitalist mode of production', namely the *real* subsumption of labour under capital. This is linked to the historical emergence of what Marx called the 'specific mode of capitalist production, namely industrial production'. Here the worker is not only paid a wage, but the work process itself is radically transformed: its phenomenology is now entirely dictated by the requirements of the self-valorization of capital, and no longer by residual traditions. Labour becomes an internal element to the capitalist production process and the worker, when entering the factory leaves his or her proper will behind and subjects to the factory discipline: 'capital absorbs labour into itself as though its body were by love possessed' (Marx, 1973[1939]: 704 – as E.P. Thompson [1968], among others, has described it was by no means easy to achieve this. Discipline the workforce was one of the greater problems of nineteenth-century industrialists, and, one might add, for the trade unions).

4 *Operaio sociale* means 'social worker' in English. This is a direct reference to Marx's term 'social individual'. In the 'Passage on Machinery' in the *Grundrisse* Marx argues that with the emergence of large scale industry, the key productive power becomes the 'general social knowledge' that is embodied in the factory environment. The worker has access to this, not on account of his individual merit, but on account of his simple existence as a social individual. '[I]t is, in a word, the development of the social individual which appears as the great foundation stone of production and of wealth' (Marx, 1973[1939]: 705). For Negri, the social worker employs the general communicative capacity that he or she has access to in virtue of his simple existence as a member of society, as a 'social individual'.

4 Brand management

1 Josiah Wedgwood to Thomas Bentley, 23 August 1772, as cited in Koehn, 2001: 34.

2 Josiah Wedgwood to Thomas Bentley, September, 1767 as cited in Koehn, 2001: 12.

5 Online branding

1 As cited in Souble, S. 2001, 'Beyond the Wireless Bubble', *FastCompany*, March, n. 44.

References

Aaker, D. 1991, *Managing Brand Equity*, New York: The Free Press.

Admap, 1966, 'Symposium for Media Executives, II', October.

Agamben, G. 1998, *Homo Sacer*, Stanford, CA: Stanford University Press.

Agamben, G. 2001, *La comunità che viene*, Turin: Bollati Boringhieri.

Alberoni, F. 1967, *Consumi e società*, Bologna: il Mulino.

Alberoni, F. and Baglioni, G. 1965, *L'integrazione del immigrato nella società industriale*, Bologna, il Mulino.

Althusser, L. 1970 (1984), 'Ideology and Ideological State Apparatuses', *Essays on Ideology*, London: Verso.

Amadori, A. 2002, *Mi consenta*, Milan: Scheiwiller.

Anderson, B. 1991, *Imagined Communities: Reflections on the Origins and Spread of Nationalism*, London: Verso.

Andrejevic, A. 2003, *Reality TV. The Work of Being Watched*, Lanham, MD: Rowman & Littlefield.

Andrejevic, M. 2002, 'The Kinder, Gentler Gaze of Big Brother: Reality in the Era of Digital Capitalism', *New Media and Society*, 4(2): pp. 251–70.

Ang, I. 1991, *Desperately Seeking the Audience*, London: Routledge.

Appadurai, A. 1986, 'Introduction', ed. Appadurai, A. *The Social Life of Things*, Cambridge: Cambridge University Press.

Appadurai, A. 1996, *Modernity at Large*, Minneapolis, MN: University of Minnesota Press.

Appadurai, A. 2002, 'Deep Democracy: Urban Governmentality and the Horizon of Politics', *Public Culture*, 14(1): pp. 21–48.

Arendt, H. 1958, *The Human Condition*, Chicago, IL: University of Chicago Press.

Arvidsson, A. 2000, 'The Therapy of Consumption: Motivation Research and the New Italian Housewife, 1958–68', *Journal of Material Culture*, 5(3): pp. 251–74.

Arvidsson, A. 2001, 'Between Fascism and the American Dream: Advertising in Interwar Italy', *Social Science History*, 25(2): pp. 152–86.

Arvidsson, A. 2003, *Marketing Modernity: Italian Advertising from Fascism to Postmodernity*, London: Routledge.

Augé, M. 1998, *Non Places: An Anthropology of Supermodernity*, London: Verso.

Bagnasco, A. 1977, *Tre Italie: La problematica territoriale dello sviluppo Italiano*, Bologna: il Mulino.

Balsinde, R., Böhmer, C., Callejo, T., Pekka-Kaukonen, H. and Pertunen, R. 2000, 'Value on the Line', *The McKinsey Quarterly*, 4.

Baran, P. and Sweezy, P.M. 1966, *Monopoly Capital*, New York: Monthly Review Press.

Barbrook, R. 1999, 'The High-Tech Gift Economy', *ReadMe! Filtered by Nettime: ASCII Culture and the Revenge of Knowledge*, New York: Autonomedia.

Barday, S. 2001, *Movie Crazy: Fans, Stars and the Cult of Celebrity*, London: Palgrave.

Bardi, L. 1996, 'Anti-Party Sentiment and Party Change in Italy', *European Journal of Political Research*, 29: pp. 343–63.

Bargh, J.A., McKenna, K.Y.A. and Fitzsimmons, G.M. 2002, 'Can You See the Real Me? Activation and Expression of the "True Self" on the Internet', *Journal of Social Issues*, 58(1): pp. 33–48.

Barnett, N.L. 1969, 'Beyond Market Segmentation', *Harvard Business Review*, January.

Barney, J. and Stewart, A. 2000, 'Organizational Identity as Moral Philosophy: Competitive Implications for Diversified Corporations', eds Hatch, M.J., Larsen, M.H. and Schultz, M. *The Expressive Organization: Linking Identity, Reputation and the Corporate Brand*, Oxford: Oxford University Press.

Barry, A. 2001, *Political Machines: Governing a Technological Society*, London: Athlone Press.

Bartels, R. 1976, *The History of Marketing Thought*, Columbus, OH: Grind.

Baudrillard, J. 1970 (2001), 'Consumer Society', ed. Poster, M. *Jean Baudrillard: Selected Writings*, Cambridge: Polity.

Bauman, Z. 1992, *Intimations of Postmodernity*, Cambridge: Polity Press.

Baym, N. 1996, 'The Emergence of Community in Computer Mediated Communication', ed. Jones, S. *Cybersociety, Computer Mediated Communication and Community*, London: Sage.

Beck, U. 1992, *Risk Society*, London: Sage.

Bedbury, S. and Fenichell, S. 2002, *A New Brand World: 8 Principles for Achieving Brand Leadership in the 21st Century*, New York: Viking.

Beller, J. 2002, 'KINO-I, KINO-WORLD. Notes on the Cinematic Mode of Production', ed. Mirzoeff, N. *The Visual Culture Reader*, London: Routledge.

Bellofiore, R., ed. 1998, *Marxian Economics: A Reappraisal*, London: Macmillan.

Belk, R. 1988, 'Possessions and the Extended Self', *Journal of Consumer Research*, 15: pp. 139–68.

Beniger, J.R. 1986, *The Control Revolution: Technological and Economic Origins of the Information Society*, Cambridge, MA: Harvard University Press.

Benjamin, W. 1983, *Das Passagen-Werk*, Frankfurt: Suhrkampf.

Benni, E., Hjartar, K. and Laartz, J. 2003, 'The IT Factor in Mobile Services', *The McKinsey Quarterly*, 3.

Berg, M. and Clifford, H., eds 1999, *Consumers and Luxury: Consumer Culture in Europe, 1650–1850*, Manchester: Manchester University Press.

Berger, W. 2001, *Advertising Today*, New York: Phaidon.

Beville, H.M. 1940, 'The ABCD's of Radio Audiences', *Public Opinion Quarterly*, June.

Black, E. 2001, *IBM and the Holocaust: The Strategic Alliance between Nazi Germany and America's most Powerful Corporation*, New York: Crown.

Blackett, T. and Russell, N. 2000, 'Co-branding: The Science of Alliance', *Journal of Brand Management*, 7(3): pp. 161–70.

Blasi, G. 1999, *Internet: Storia e futuro di un nuovo medium*, Milan: Guerini Studi.

Bocca-Altieri, G. 2004, *I media-mondo: Forme e linguaggi dell'esperienza contemporanea*, Rome: Meltempi.

Bogart, L. 1963, 'Inside Market Research', *Public Opinion Quarterly*, 27(4): pp. 562–77.

Bogart, L. 1966, 'Is it Time to Discard the Audience Concept?', *Journal of Marketing*, 80: pp. 47–54.

Bogart, L. 1987, Review: Bourdieu, P. 'Distinction', *Public Opinion Quarterly*, 51(1): pp. 131–4.

Boltanski, L. and Chiapello, E. 1999, *Le nouvel esprit du capitalisme*, Paris: Gallimard.

Bonner, F. and du Gay, P. 1992, 'Representing the Enterprising Self: Thirty-something and Contemporary Consumer Culture', *Theory Culture and Society*, 9: pp. 67–92.

Bourdieu, P. 1984, *Distinction*, London: Routledge.

Bowlby, R. 1985, *Just Looking: Consumer Culture in Dreisser, Gissing and Zola*, London: Methuen.

Bowlby, R. 2000, *Carried Away: The Invention of Modern Shopping*, London: Faber & Faber.

Braff, A., Passmore, W. and Simpson, M. 2003, 'Going the Distance with Telecom Customers', *The McKinsey Quarterly*, 4.

Braudel, F. 1985, *La dynamique du capitalisme*, Paris: Arthaud.

Brewer, J. 1997, *The Pleasures of the Imagination: English Culture in the Eighteenth Century*, London: HarperCollins.

Brewer, J. and Porter, R., eds 1993, *Consumption and the World of Goods*, New York: Routledge.

Brickner, B. 2003, 'Clash of Communities: A Study of the Lego Product Bionicle', Working paper, MODINET, University of Copenhagen, www.modinet.dk.

British Bureau of Market Research, 1961, 'Trends in Food and Cooking Habits', unpublished report, box 577, J. Walter Thompson Collection, History of Advertising Trust, Ravenningham, Norwich, UK.

Broadbent, S. 1967, 'Qualitative Factors and Media Selection', *Admap*, June.

Burnett, R. 1996, *Global Jukebox: The International Music Industry*, London: Routledge.

Callon, M., ed. 1998, *The Laws of Markets*, Oxford: Blackwell.

Campbell, C. 1987, *The Romanic Ethic and the Spirit of Modern Consumerism*, Oxford: Blackwell.

Carew, A. 1987, *Labour under the Marshall Plan: The Politics of Productivity and the Marketing of Management Science*, Manchester: Manchester University Press.

Carrier, J.G. and Miller, D., eds 1998, *Virtualism: A New Political Economy*, Oxford: Berg.

Carter, M. 2002, 'Branding Takes the Road Test', *Financial Times*, 17 April.

Castells, M. 1996, *The Information Age*, vol. I, Oxford: Blackwell.

Castells, M. 2001, *The Internet Galaxy*, Oxford: Oxford University Press.

Celsi, R., Rose, R. and Leigh, T. 1993, 'An Exploration of High-risk Leisure Consumption through Sky-diving', *Journal of Consumer Research*, 20: pp. 1–21.

Chaffee, S. 1985, 'Popular Music and Communication Research', *Communication Research*, 12: 413–24.

Chasin, A. 2000, *Selling Out: The Gay and Lesbian Movement Goes to Market*, London: Palgrave.

Cherington, P.T. 1924, 'Statistics in Market Research', *Annals of the American Academy of Political and Social Science*, 115: pp. 130–5.

Cherny, L. and Wese, E.R., eds 1996, *Wired Women*, London: Airlife Book Company.

Clarke, J., Hall, S., Jefferson, T. and Roberts, B. 1975, 'Subcultures, Cultures and Class: A Theoretical Overview', eds Hall, S. and Jefferson, T., *Resistance through Rituals*, London: Hutchinson.

Cochoy, F. 1999, *Une histoire du marketing*, Paris: Editions de la Decouverte.

Cohen, L. 1990, *Making a New Deal: Industrial Workers in Chicago 1919–1939*, Cambridge: Cambridge University Press.

Comaroff, J. and Comaroff, J. 2000, 'Millennial Capitalism: First Thoughts on a Second Coming', *Public Culture*, 12(2): pp. 291–343.

Converse, J.M. 1987, *Survey Research in the United States, its Roots and Emergence, 1890–1960*, Berkeley, CA: University of California Press.

Coontz, S. 1992, *The Way We Never Were*, New York: HarperCollins.

Cova, B. 1997, 'Community and Consumption: Towards a Theory of the Linking Value of Products and Services', *European Journal of Marketing*, 31(3/4).

Cova, B. and Cova, V. 2001, 'Tribal Aspects of Postmodern Consumption Research: The Case of French In-line Roller Skaters', *Journal of Consumer Behaviour*, 1: pp. 67–76.

Cowley, D. 1999, 'Introduction', ed. Cowley, D. *Understanding Brands*, London: Kogan Page.

Cunningham, T. 2002, Interview, *The Merchants of Cool*, www.pbs.org/wgbh/pages/frontline/shows/cool/interviews/cunningham, 12 September 2002.

Curtin, M. 1996, 'On the Edge: The Culture Industries in the Neo Network Era', ed. Ohmann, R. *Making and Selling Culture*, Hannover, NH: Wesleyian University Press.

Davenport, T. and Beck, J. 2001, *The Attention Economy: Understanding the New Currency of Business*, Cambridge, MA: Harvard Business School Press.

Davies, D. ed. 2000, *The Consumer Revolution in Urban China*, Berkeley, CA: University of California Press.

Dean, M. 1999, *Governmentality*, London: Sage.

De Certeau, M. 1984, *The Practice of Everyday Life*, Berkeley, CA: University of California Press.

de Graaf, S. and Nieborg, D. 2003, 'Together we Brand: America's Army', eds Copier, M. and Raessens, J. *Level Up: Digital Games Research Conference, 4–6 November 2003*, Utrecht: DIGRA.

de Grazia, V. 1992, *How Mussolini Ruled Italian Women*, Berkeley, CA: University of California Press.

Demby, E. 1974, 'Psychographics: From Whence it Came', ed. Wells, D.W. *Life Style and Psychographics*, Chicago, IL: American Marketing Association.

Denizen, N. 2001, 'The Seventh Moment: Qualitative Inquiry and the Practices of a More Radical Consumer Research', *Journal of Consumer Research*, 28(2): pp. 324–30.

Desjardins, M. 1999, 'Lucy and Desi: Sexuality, Ethnicity, and TV's First Family', eds Haralovich, M.B. and Rabinovitz, L. *Television, History and American Culture: Critical Feminist Essays,* Durham, NC: Duke University Press.

Deutsch, K. 1953, *Nationalism and Social Communication*, Cambridge, MA: MIT Press.

De Vries, J. 1993, 'Between Purchasing Power and the World of Goods: Understanding the Household Economy in Early Modern Europe', eds Brewer J. and Porter R. *Consumption and the World of Goods*, New York: Routledge.

Diamanti, I. 2003, *Bianco, rosso verde e azzurro, Mappe e colori dell Italia politica*, Bologna: il Mulino.

Dibbel, J. 1997, 'A Rape in Cyberspace: How an Evil Clown, a Haitian Trickster Spirit, Two Wizards and Cast of Dozens Turned a Database into a Society', ed. Stefik, M. *Internet Dreams: Archetypes, Myths and Metaphors*, Cambridge, MA: MIT Press.

Dichter, E. 1949, 'A Psychological View of Advertising Effectiveness', *Journal of Marketing*, XIV(1): pp. 62–6.

Dichter, E. 1960, *The Strategy of Desire*, London, New York: Boardman & Co.

Dichter, E. 1965, 'Discovering the Inner Joneses', *Harvard Business Review*, May–June.

Digg, A.T. 1966, 'Lintas in Computerland', *Admap*, December.

Donn, J.E. and Sherman, R.C. 2002, 'Attitudes and Practices Regarding the Formation of Romantic Relationships on the Internet', *Cyberpsychology & Behaviour*, 5: pp. 107–23.

Douglas, M. and Isherwood, B. 1979, *The World of Goods*, London: Allen Cone.

D'Souza, S. 1986, 'What is Account Planning?', www.apg.org.uk/Content/ WhatIsPlanning.htm.

Duesenberry, J.S. 1949, *Income, Savings and the Theory of Consumer Behaviour*, New York: Oxford University Press.

du Gay, P. 1996, *Consumption and Identity at Work*, London: Sage.

Dyer-Withford, N. 1999, *Cyber-Marx: Cycles and Circuits of Struggle in High Technology Capitalism*, Urbana, IL: University of Illinois Press,

The Economist, 1999, 'Survey of Telecommunications', 9 October.

Ehrenreich, B. 1990, *Fear of Falling*, New York: Harper.

Elliott, R. and Wattanasuwan, K. 1998, 'Brands as Symbolic Resources for the Construction of Identity', *International Journal of Advertising*, 17(2).

Emmison, R. 2003, 'Social Class and Cultural Mobility: Reconfiguring the Cultural Omnivore Thesis', *Journal of Sociology*, 39(3): pp. 211–30.

Enzenberger, H.M. 1970, 'Constituents of a Theory of the Media', *New Left Review*, 64: pp. 13–36.

Ewen, S. 1976, *Captains of Consciousness*, New York: McGraw-Hill.

Export Advertiser, 1930, Advertisement: 'Cinelandia', July, p. 25.

Eyerman, R. and Jamison, A. 1994, *Seeds of the Sixties*, Berkeley, CA: University of California Press.

Featherstone, M. 1991, *Consumer Culture and Postmodernism*, London: Sage.

Featherstone, M. and Burrows, R., eds 1995, *Cyberspace, Cyberbodies, Cyberpunk: Cultures of Technological Embodiment*, London: Routledge.

Feldwick, P. 1999, 'Defining a Brand', ed. Cowley, D. *Understanding Brands – By 10 People who Do*, London: Kogan Page.

Finn, M. 2004, 'Gifted Commodities East and West: Family Politics and the Exchange of Goods in Britain and British India, *c.* 1790–1830', Paper presented at the conference, *Consumption Modernity and the West*, Pasadena, CA, 16–17 April 2004.

Firat, A.F. and Dholakia, N. 1998, *Consuming People: From Political Economy to Theatres of Consumption*, London: Routledge.

Firat, A.F. and Schutz, C. 1997, 'From Segmentation to Fragmentation: Markets and Marketing in the Postmodern Era', *European Journal of Marketing*, 31(3/4): pp. 183–207.

Firat, A.F. and Venkatesh, A. 1995, 'Liberatory Postmodernism and the Re-enchantment of Consumption', *Journal of Consumer Research*, 22: pp. 239–67.

Fisher, T., Brown, M. and Wightman, D. 1968, 'People are Different', *Admap*, January.

Fomburn, C.J. and Rindova, V. 2000, 'The Road to Transparency: Reputation Management at Royal Dutch/Shell', eds Hatch, M.J., Larsen, M.H. and Schultz, M. *The Expressive Organization: Linking Identity, Reputation and the Corporate Brand*, Oxford: Oxford University Press.

Foucault, M. 1972, *The Archaeology of Knowledge*, New York: Pantheon.

Foucault, M. 1975, *Surveiller et punir*, Paris: Gallimard.

Foucault, M. 1991, 'Governmentality', eds Burchell, G. and Gordon, C. *The Foucault Effect: Studies in Governmentality*, London: Harvester Wheatsheaf.

Fourier, S. 1998, 'Consumers and their Brands: Developing Relationship Theory in Consumer Research', *Journal of Consumer Research*, 24(4): pp. 343–73.

Fox, S. 1984, *The Mirror Makers: A History of American Advertising and its Creators*, New York: William Morrow & Co.

Frank, T. 1999, *One Market under God*, Chicago, IL: University of Chicago Press.

Franklin, S., Lury, C. and Stacey, J. 2000, *Global Nature, Global Culture*, London: Routledge.

French, P. 1998, *One Billion Shoppers. Accessing Asia's Consuming Passions and Fast Moving Markets After the Meltdown*, London: Brealy.

Fuglesang, M. 1994, *Veils and Videos: Female Youth Culture on the Kenyan Coast*, Stockholm Studies in Anthropology.

Fuller, J., Bartel, M., Ernst, H. and Muhbaker, H. 2004, 'Community Brand Innovation: A Method to Utilize the Innovative Potential of Online Communities', *Proceedings of the 37th International Conference on System Sciences*.

Fullerton, R. 1988, 'How Modern is Modern Marketing? Marketing's Evolution and the Myth of the Producton Era', *Journal of Marketing*, 52: pp. 108–25.

Gad, T. 2000, *4-D Branding: Cracking the Corporate Code of the Network*, Stockholm: Bookuser.

Gandy, O. 1993, *The Panoptic Sort: A Political Economy of Personal Information*, Boulder, CO: Westview Press.

Gans, H. 1966, 'Popular Culture in America', ed. Becker, H. *Social Problems: A Modern Approach*, New York: Wiley.

Gardner, B. and Levy, S. 1955, 'The Product and the Brand', *Harvard Business Review*, March–April: pp. 33–9.

Gates, B. 1996, *The Road Ahead*, London, Penguin.

Gérin, O.J. and Éspinadel, C. 1911, *La publicité suggestive*, Paris: Dunod & Pinad.

Gerke, S. 2000, 'Global Lifestyles under Local Conditons: The New Indonesian Middle Class', ed. Beng-Huat, L. *Consumption in Asia: Lifestyles and Identities*, London: Routledge.

Ghosh, R.A. 1999, 'Cooking-Pot Markets: An Economic Model for the Trade in Free Goods and Services on the Internet', *ReadMe! Filtered by Nettime. ASCII Culture and the Revenge of Knowledge*, New York: Autonomedia.

Giddens, A. 1991, *Modernity and Self Identity*, Cambridge: Polity Press.

Ginsborg, P. 2004, *Silvio Berlusconi: Television, Power and Patrimony*, London: Verso.

Gladwell, M. 1997, 'The Coolhunt', *The New Yorker*, 17 March.

Gladwell, M. 2002, *The Tipping Point: How Little Things Can Make a Big Difference*, Boston, MA: Little, Brown.

Glick, I. and Levy, S. 1962, *Living with Television*, Chicago, IL: Aldine.

Gobe, M. 2001, *Emotional Branding: The New Paradigm for Connecting Brands to People*, New York: Allworth.

Godin, S. 2000, 'Unleash your Ideavirus', *Fast Company*, August.

Goffman, E. 1974, *Frame Analysis*, Harmondsworth: Penguin.

Goldman, R. and Papson. S. 1996, *Nike Culture*, London: Sage.

Goodchild, J. and Callow, C., eds 2001, *Brands: Visions and Values*, New York: Wiley.

Gordon, W. 1999, *Goodthinking: A Guide to Qualitative Research*, Henley-on-Thames: Admap.

Gorz, A. 2003, *L'immatériel*, Paris: Galilée.

Graham, J. 2003, 'Match.com: Love at First Click', *Brandchannel* (www.brandchannel.com), 12 February.

Gramsci, A. 1971, 'Americanism and Fordism', eds Hoare, Q. and Nowell Smith, G. *Selections from the Prison Notebooks*, New York: International Publishers.

Grant, J. 1999, *The New Marketing Manifesto*, New York: Texre.

Green, N. 2002, 'On the Move: Technology, Mobility, and the Mediation of Social Time and Space', *The Information Society*, 18: pp. 281–92.

Grodal, T. 1997, *Moving Pictures*, Oxford: Clarendon Press.

Grossman, L. 2003, 'The Quest for Cool', Time.com, 31 August.

Habermas, J. 1989, *The Structural Transformation of the Public Sphere*, Boston, MA: Beacon.

Hage, J. and Powers, C.H. 1992, *Post-Industrial Lives: Roles and Relationships in the 21st Century*, London: Sage.

Hagel, J. and Armstrong, A. 1997, *Net.gain: Expanding Markets through Virtual Communities*, Boston, MA: Harvard Business School Press.

Haggerty, K.D. and Ericsson, R.V. 2000, 'The Surveillant Assemblage', *British Journal of Sociology*, 51(4): pp. 605–22.

Haig, M. 2002, *Mobile Marketing: The Message Revolution*, London: Kogan Page.

Hall, S. and Jefferson, T., eds 1975, *Resistance through Rituals*, London: Hutchinson.

Hamilton, D. and Kirby, K. 2002, 'A New Brand for a New Category: Paint It Orange', *Design Management Journal*, Winter: pp. 41–5.

Hannerz, U. 1992, *Cultural Complexity*, New York: Columbia University Press.

Hannerz, U. 1996, *Transnational Connections*, London: Routledge.

Hardt, M. and Negri, A. 2004, *Multitude*, London: Penguin.

Hardy, H. 1993, *History of the Internet*, Master's Thesis, School of Communications, Grand Valley State University, Allendale, MI.

Harries, D. 2002, *The New Media Book*, London: bfi Publishing.

Harvey, D. 1990, *The Condition of Postmodernity*, Oxford: Blackwell.

Hatfield, S. 1993, 'Generation X, Advertising's Nightmare', *Campaign*, 26 November.

Hebdidge, D. 1979, *Subculture: The Meaning of Style*, London: Methuen.

Heelas, P. 2002, 'Work Ethics, Soft Capitalism and the "Turn to Life"', eds du Gay, P. and Pryke, M. *Cultural Economy*, London: Sage.

Heidegger, M. 1935(1971) *The Origin of the Work of Art,* New York: HarperCollins.

Hesmondhalgh, D. 2002, *The Cultural Industries,* London: Sage.

Higgins, D. 1965, *The Art of Writing Advertising: Conversations with Masters of the Craft,* Chicago, IL: NTC Business Books.

Hilton, M. 2000, *Smoking in British Popular Culture, 1800–2000,* Manchester: Manchester University Press.

Himanen, P. 2001, *The Hacker Ethic and the Spirit of the Information Age,* London: Vintage.

Hine, T. 1986, *Populux,* New York: Knopf.

Hochschild, A.R. 1997, *The Time Bind: When Work becomes Home and Home Becomes Work,* New York: Metropolitan Books.

Hoggart, R. 1957, *The Uses of Literacy,* London: Penguin.

Hollander, S. 1992, *Was there a Pepsi Generation before Pepsi Discovered it? Youth Based Segmentation in Marketing,* New York: NTC Business Books.

Holt, D.B. 1997, 'Poststructuralist Lifestyle Analysis: Conceptualizing the Social Patterning of Consumption in Postmodernity', *Journal of Consumer Research,* 23(4): pp. 326–50.

Holt, D.B. 2002, 'Why do Brands Cause Trouble? A Dialectical Theory of Consumer Culture and Branding', *Journal of Consumer Research,* 29: pp. 70–90.

Horkheimer, M. and Adorno, T. 1944 (1972) *The Dialectic of Enlightenment,* York: Seabury Press.

Hutchby, I. 2001, 'Technologies, Texts, Affordances', *Sociology,* 35(2): pp. 441–56.

Ind, N. and Rondino, M.C. 2001, 'Branding the Web: A Real Revolution', *Journal of Brand Management,* 9(1): pp. 8–19.

James, E.P.H. 1937, 'The Development of Research in Broadcast Advertising', *The Journal of Marketing,* 2: pp. 141–5.

Jameson, F. 1991, *Postmodernism, or The Cultural Logic of Late Capitalism,* Durham, NC: Duke University Press.

Janson, A. 2002, 'The Mediatization of Consumer Culture: Towards an Analytical Framework of Image Culture', *Journal of Consumer Culture,* 2(1): pp. 5–31.

Jauréguiberry, F. 2000, 'Mobile Telecommunications and the Management of Time', *Social Science Information,* 39(2): pp. 255–68.

Jensen, J. 1999, 'Interactivity: Tracing a New Concept in Media and Communication Studies', *Nordicom Review,* 19(1): pp. 185–204.

Joachimsthaler, E. and Aaker, D.A. 1997, 'Building Brands Without Mass Media', *Harvard Business Review,* January/February.

Jones, G. 1992, *Honey, I'm Home. Sitcoms: Selling the American Dream,* New York: St. Martin's Press.

Jurveson, J. and Draper, T. 1998, 'Viral Marketing', *Business 2.0,* November (also available at www.djf.com/files/viralmarketing.htm).

JWT, 1928, 'Mr Resor Leads Discussion on Personality Advertising', *J.W.T. Newsletter*, 13/4, 1928, J. Walter Thompson Collection, Special Collections Library, Duke University, NC.

JWT, 1929, 'Representatives Meeting, 3/12, 1929', J. Walter Thompson Collection, Special Collections Library, Duke University, NC.

JWT, 1935a, 'Little Stories Behind the Accounts: Lux Flakes 1', *J.W.T. Newsletter*, 12/4, 1935, J. Walter Thompson Collection, Special Collections Library, Duke University, NC.

JWT, 1935b, 'Little Stories Behind the Accounts: Lux Flakes 2', *J.W.T. Newsletter*, 15/5, 1935, J. Walter Thompson Collection, Special Collections Library, Duke University, NC.

JWT, 1957, 'Interurbia: The Changing Face of America', Publications, box 18, J. Walter Thompson Collection, Special Collections Library, Duke University, NC.

Kasesniemi, E. and Rautiainen, P. 2002, 'Mobile Culture of Children and Teenagers in Finland', eds Katz, J.E. and Aakhus, M. *Perpetual Contact: Mobile Communication, Private Talk, Public Performance,* Cambridge: Cambridge University Press.

Kates, S.M. 1998, *Twenty Million New Consumers! Understanding Gay Men's Consumer Behaviour*, Birmingham, NY: Hamilton Park.

Kates, S.M. 2002, 'The Protean Quality of Subcultural Consumption: An Ethnograpic Account of Gay Consumers', *Journal of Consumer Research*, 29(3): pp. 383–99.

Katz, J.E. and Aakhus, M. 2002, 'Introduction: Framing the Issues', eds Katz, J.E. and Aakhus, M. *Perpetual Contact: Mobile Communication, Private Talk, Public Performance*, Oxford: Oxford University Press.

Keith, R.J. 1960 (1988), 'The Marketing Revolution', *Journal of Marketing*, January (republished in eds Enis, B. and Cox, K.K. *Marketing Classics*, Boston, MA: Allyn & Bacon).

Keller, K.L. 1993, 'Conceptualizing, Measuring and Managing Customer-based Brand Equity', *Journal of Marketing*, 57(1): pp. 1–23.

Keller, K.L. 2001, 'Building Customer-based Brand Equity', *Marketing Management*, 10(2): pp. 14–19.

Kellner, D. 1995, *Media Culture: Cultural Studies, Identity and Politics between the Modern and the Postmodern*, London: Routledge.

Klein, N. 2000, *No Logo*, London: Flamingo.

Koehn, N. 2001, *Brand New*, Boston, MA: Harvard Business School Press.

Kollock, P. and Smith, M. 1996, 'Managing the Virtual Commons: Cooperation and Conflict in Computer Communities', ed. Herring, S. *Computer Mediated Communication, Linguistic, Social and Cross Cultural Perspectives*, Amsterdam: John Benjamin.

Kozinets, R. 2001, 'Utopian Enterprise: Articulating the Meanings of *Star Trek*'s Culture of Consumption', *Journal of Consumer Research*, 28: pp. 67–88.

Kreshel, P. 1989, *Towards a Cultural History of Advertising Research: A Case Study of J. Walter Thompson, 1908–25*, Ph.D. Thesis, Dept of Communications, University of Illinois at Urbana-Champaign.

Kuchta, D. 1996, 'The Making of the Self-made Man: Class, Clothing and English Masculinity, 1688–1832', eds de Grazia, V. and Furlong, E. *The Sex of Things, Gender and Consumption in Historical Perspective*, Berkeley, CA: University of California Press.

Lash, S. 2002, *Critique of Information*, London: Sage.

Lash, S. and Urry, J. 1994, *Economies of Signs and Spaces*, London: Sage.

Laufer, R. and Paradeise, C. 1990, *Marketing Democracy: Public Opinion and Media Formation in Democratic Societies*, London: Transaction Books.

Lazarsfeldt, P. 1938, 'The Panel as a New Tool for Measuring Opinion', *Public Opinion Quarterly*, 2(4): pp. 596–612.

Lazzarato, M. 1997, *Lavoro immateriale: Forme di vita e produzione di soggettività*, Verona: Ombre corte.

Lears, T.J. 1994, *Fables of Abundance*, New York: Basic Books.

Lee, B. and LiPuma, E. 2002, 'Cultures of Circulation: The Imaginations of Modernity', *Social Text, Public Culture*, 14(1): pp. 191–213.

Lee, S. and Gordon, D. 2002, 'Interview' Frontline: The Merchants of Cool, http://www.pbs.org/wgbh/pages/frontline/shows/cool/interviews/gordonandlee.html, 20/8/2004.

Lester, M.C. 2003, 'Top 5 Worst Personal Ads: What NOT to Do'. www.match.com/Matchscene/article.asp, 11/5/2003.

Levi Martin, J. 1999, 'The Myth of the Consumption Oriented Economy and the Rise of the Desiring Subject', *Theory and Society*, 28: pp. 425–53.

Levy, P. 1998, *Becoming Virtual: Reality in the Digital Age*, New York: Plenum Trade.

Levy, S. 1964, 'Symbolism and Life Style', ed. Greyser, S.A. *Toward Scientific Marketing*, Proceedings of the Winter Conference of the American Marketing Association, 27–28 December 1963, Boston, MA, Chicago, IL: American Marketing Association.

Lindemann, J. 2003, 'The Financial Value of Brands', eds Clifton, R. and Simmons, J. *Brands and Branding*, London: The Economist.

Lindgren, M., Jedbratt, J. and Svensson, E. 2002, *Beyond Mobile: People, Communications and Marketing in a Mobilized World*, London: Palgrave.

Ling, R. and Ytri, B. 2002, 'Hyper-coordination via Mobile Phones in Norway', eds Katz, J.E. and Aakhus, M. *Perpetual Contact: Mobile Communication, Private Talk, Public Performance*, Cambridge: Cambridge University Press.

Lipset, S.M. 1963, *Political Man*, Garden City, NJ: Doubleday.

Lochlann, J. 2002, 'Urban Errands: The Means of Mobility', *Journal of Consumer Culture*, 2(3): 385–404.

Lockley, L. 1950, 'Notes on the History of Marketing Research', *The Journal of Marketing*, 14: 733–6.

Longhurst, B. 1995, *Popular Music and Society*, Cambridge: Polity Press.

Luhmann, N. 1979, *Trust and Power*, Chichester: John Wiley.

Luhmann, N. 1990, 'Meaning as Sociology's Basic Concept', in Luhmann, N. *Essays on Self-Reference*, New York: Columbia University Press.

Luhmann, N. 1995, *Social Systems*, Stanford, CA: Stanford University Press.

Lukács, G. 1971, *History and Class Consciousness*, London: Merlin Press.

Lumley, R. 1990, *States of Emergency: Cultures of Revolt in Italy from 1968–78*, London: Verso.

Lury, C. 1999, 'Marking Time with Nike: The Illusion of the Durable', *Public Culture*, 11(3): pp. 499–526.

Lury, C. 2004, *Brands: The Logos of the Global Economy*, London: Routledge.

McAlexander, J.H. and Shouten, J.W. 1998, 'Brandfests: Servicescapes for the Cultivation of Brand Equity', ed. Sherry, J. *Servicescapes: The Concept of Place in Contemporary Markets*, Chicago, IL: NTC Business Books.

McCarthy, A. 2001, *Ambience Television: Visual Culture and Public Space*, Durham, NC: Duke University Press.

McChesney, R. 1999, *Rich Media, Poor Democracy: Communications Politics in Dubious Times*, Urbana, IL: University of Illinois Press.

McCourt, T. and Buckhart, P. 2003, 'When Creators, Corporations and Consumers Collide: Napster and the Development of On-line Music Distribution', *Media, Culture & Society*, 25(3): pp. 333–50.

McFeely, M.D. 2000, *Can She Bake a Cherry Pie: American Women and the Kitchen in the Twentieth Century*, Amherst, MA: University of Massachusetts Press.

McGregor, D. 1960, *The Human Side of Enterprise*, New York: McGraw-Hill.

McGuigan, J. 1992, *Cultural Populism*, London: Routledge.

McKenna, K.Y.A., Green, A.S. and Gleason, M.E.J. 2002, 'Relationship Formation on the Internet: What's the Big Attraction?', *Journal for Social Issues*, 58(1): pp. 9–31.

McLuhan, M. 1964, *Understanding Media: the Extensions of Man*, London: Routledge.

McRobbie, A. 1990, *Feminism and Youth Culture, from 'Jackie' to 'Just Seventeen'*, Boston, MA: Unwin Hyman.

McWilliam, G. 2000, 'Building Strong Brands Through Online Communities', *Sloan Management Review*, Spring: pp. 43–54.

Maffesoli, M. 1996, *The Time of the Tribes,* London: Sage.

Maiser, R. 1973, 'The Decline of the Mass Audience', *Public Opinion Quarterly*, 37(2): pp. 159–70.

Malinowski, B. 1932, *The Sexual Life of Savages*, London: Routledge.

Mandel, E. 1975, *Late Capitalism*, London: New Left Books.

Manovich, L. 2001, *The Language of the New Media*, Cambridge, MA: MIT Press.

Maravelias, C. 2003, 'Post-bureacracy: Control through Professional Freedom', *Journal of Organizational Change Management*, 16(5): pp. 547–66.

Marazzi, C. 1999a, *E il denaro va*,Turin: Bollati Boringhieri.

Marazzi, C. 1999b, *Il posto dei calzini: La svolta linguistica dell'economia e i suoi effetti sulla politica*, Turin: Bollati Boringhieri.

Marchand, R. 1985, *Advertising the American Dream: Making Way for Modernity, 1920–40*, Berkeley, CA: University of California Press.

Marchand, R. 1998, *Creating the Corporate Soul*, Berkeley, CA: University of California Press.

Marling, K.A. 1994, *As Seen on TV: The Visual Culture of the American Home in the 1950s*, Boston, MA: Harvard University Press.

Marshall, P.D. 2002, 'The New Inter-textual Commodity', ed. Harries, D. *The New Media Book*, London: British Film Institute.

Martineau, P. 1957, *Motivation in Advertising*, New York: McGraw-Hill.

Marwick, A. 1998, *The Sixties*, Oxford: Oxford University Press.

Marx, 1973 (1939), *Grundrisse*, London: Penguin.

Marx, 1990 (1867), *Capital, vol. I*, London: Penguin.

Maslow, A.H. 1954, *Motivation and Personality*, New York: Harper.

Mattelart, A. 1991, *Advertising International*, London: Routledge.

Mauss, M. 1954, *The Gift*, Glencoe: The Free Press.

Meikle, J.L. 1995, *American Plastic: A Cultural History*, New Brunswick, NJ: Rutgers University Press.

Middleton, R. 1990, *Studying Popular Music*, Milton Keynes: Open University Press.

Miller, D. 1995, 'Consumption as the Vanguard of History: A Polemic by Way of an Introduction', ed. Miller, D. *Acknowledging Consumption: A Review of New Studies*, London: Routledge.

Miller, D. 1997, *Capitalism: An Ethnographic Approach*, Oxford: Berg.

Miller, D. 1998, *A Theory of Shopping*, Cambridge: Polity Press.

Mills, C.W. 1951, *White Collar: The American Middle Classes*, Oxford: Oxford University Press.

Miranda, J. 1998, 'The Performance of Consumption and Production', *Social Text,* 54(10): pp. 25–68.

Morin, E. 1967, *Commune en France: La métamorphose de Plodémet*, Paris.

Morris, M. 1992, 'On the Beach', eds Grossberg, L., Nelson, C. and Treichler, P., *Cultural Studies*, London: Routledge.

Morris-Suzuki, T. 1984, 'Robots and Captialism', *New Left Review*, 147(I): pp. 109–21.

Morris-Suzuki, T. 1997, 'Capitalism in the Computer Age', eds Davis, J., Hirschl, T. and Stack, M. *Cutting Edge: Technology, Society and Social Revolution*, London: Verso.

Mort, F. 1996, *Cultures of Consumption: Masculinity and Social Space in Late Twentieth Century Britain*, London: Routledge.

Motivations, 1956a, 'What the New Rich Americans Really Want to Buy', July.

Motivations, 1956b, 'Something Must Be Added', June.

Motivations, 1957, 'The Emotional Plus in Suburban Living', June.

Moulier-Boutang, Y. 1998, *De l'esclavage au salariat. Économie historique du salariat bridé*, Paris, Puf.

Moulier-Boutang, Y., ed. 2002, *L'età del capitalismo cognitivo*, Verona: Ombre Corte.

Mukerji, C. 1983, *From Graven Images: Patterns of Modern Materialism*, New York: Columbia University Press.

Muniz, A. and O'Guinn, T. 2001, 'Brand Community', *Journal of Consumer Research*, 27(4): pp. 412–32.

Murdoch, G. 2000, 'Digital Futures: European Television in the Age of Convergence', eds Wieten, J., Murdoch, G. and Dahlgren, P. *Television Across Europe*, London: Sage.

Murphy, J. 2001, *Brand Valuation: Establishing a True and Fair View*, London: Business Books.

Murray, J. 1997, *Hamlet on the Holodeck: The Future of Narrative in Cyberspace*, Cambridge, MA: MIT Press.

Nava, M. 1997, 'The Framing of Advertising', eds Nava, M., Blake, A., MacRury, I. and Richards, B. *Buy this Book: Studies in Advertising and Consumption*, London: Routledge.

Negri, A. 1989, *The Politics of Subversion. A Manifesto for the Twenty-first Century*, Cambridge: Polity Press.

Negri, A. 1996, 'Twenty Theses on Marx', eds Makdisi, S., Casarino, C. and Karl, R., *Marxism Beyond Marxism*, London: Routledge.

Negri, A. 1999, 'Value and Affect', *Boundary 2*, 26(2): pp. 77–88.

Negroponte, N. 1995, *Being Digital*, London, Hodder & Stoughton.

Nixon, S. 1996, *Hard Looks: Masculinities, Spectatorship and Contemporary Consumption*, London: UCL Press.

Nixon, S. 2003, *Advertising Cultures*, London: Sage.

Norton, D.W. and Hansen, L. 2001, 'The E-commerce Development: Creating Online Brand Experiences', *Design Management Journal*, 11(4): pp. 25–42.

Nuttall, C. 2003, 'Everything to Play For', Special Report, *Financial Times* 10 December.

Nye, R. 1975, *The Origins of Crowd Psychology: Gustave LeBon and the Crisis of Mass Democracy in the Third Republic*, London: Sage.

Oddy, D.J. 2003, *From Plain Fare to Fusion Food: British Diet from the 1890s to the 1990s*, Woodbridge: The Boydell Press.

O'Guinn, T. and Belk, R. 1989, 'Heaven on Earth: Consumption at Heritage Village, USA', *Journal of Consumer Research*, 16: pp. 227–38.

Ohmann, R. 1996, *Selling Culture: Magazines, Markets and Class at the Turn of the Century*, London: Verso.

Olijnyk, Z. 2002, 'Matchmaker, Matchmaker, Make Me a Bundle', *Canadian Business*, 75(3): pp. 54–61.

Olins, W. 2000, 'How Brands are Taking Over the Corporation', eds Hatch, M.J., Larsen, M.H. and Schultz, M. *The Expressive Organization: Linking Identity, Reputation and the Corporate Brand*, Oxford: Oxford University Press.

Osgerby, B. 2001, *Playboys in Paradise: Masculinity, Youth and Leisure Style in Modern America*, Oxford: Berg.

Paolucci, C. and Barbesino, P. 1995, *The Shift to Postmodern Political Representation in Italy*, Working Paper EUI, Florence.

Paranara, S. 1958, 'Marketing Implications of Interurban Development', publications, box 18, J. Walter Thompson Collection, Special Collections Library, Duke University, NC.

Parks, M. and Floyd, K. 1996, 'Making Friends in Cyberspace', *Journal of Communication,* Winter.

Parsons, T. 1942 (1964), 'Age and Sex in the Social Structure of the United States', *Essays in Sociological Theory,* Glencoe, IL: The Free Press.

Pattersen, M. 1999, 'Re-appraising the Concept of Brand Image', *Journal of Brand Management,* 6(6): pp. 409–26.

Pegram, B. and Acreman, S. 2000, 'Breathing Life into Research Data', *Admap,* January.

Peiss, K. 1986, *Cheap Amusements: Working Women and Leisure in Turn of the Century New York,* Philadelphia, PA: Temple University Press.

Peñaloza, L. 1999, 'Just Doing it: A Visual Ethnographic Study of Spectacular Consumption Behaviour at Nike Town', *Consumption, Markets & Culture,* 2(4): pp. 337–400.

Peretti, J. 2001, 'My Nike Media Adventure', *The Nation,* 22 March.

Perry, M., O'Hara, K., Sellen, A., Brown, B. and Harper, R. 2001, 'Dealing with Mobility: Understanding Access Anytime, Anywhere', *Transactions on Human–Computer Interaction,* 8(4): 323–47.

Peters, J.D. 1999, *Speaking into the Air: A History of the Idea of Communication,* Chicago, IL: University of Chicago Press.

Pettinger, L. 2004, 'Brand Culture and Branded Workers: Service Work and Aesthetic Labour in Fashion Retail', *Consumption, Markets and Culture,* 7(2): pp. 165–84.

Pine, J.P. and Gilmore, J.H. 1999, *The Experience Economy: Work is Theatre and Everyday Business is a Stage,* Boston, MA: Harvard Business School Press.

Piore, M. and Sabel, C.F. 1984, *The Second Industrial Divide,* New York: Basic Books.

Plant, S. 1997, *Zeros and Ones: Digital Women and the New Technoculture,* London: Fourth Estate.

Pole, S. 2000, *Trigger Happy: The Inner Life of Videogames,* London: Fourth Estate.

Polhemus, T. 1994, *Street Styles,* London: Victoria and Albert Museum.

Pollitt, S. 1979, 'How I Started Account Planning in the Sixties', *Campaign,* April.

Poropudas, T. 2002a, 'An Image Turns Out to be the Mobile Killer Application', Mobile CommerceNet (www.mobile.commerce.net), 22 August.

Poropudas, T. 2002b, 'Analysts Predict a Strong Gaming Trend', Mobile CommerceNet (www.mobile.commerce.net), 7 December.

Poropudas, T. 2002c, 'Nokia Plays Game With Koreans', Mobile CommerceNet (www.mobile.commerce.net), 29 August.

Poutain, D. and Robins, D. 2000, *Cool Rules: Anatomy of an Attitude,* London: Reaktion Books.

Predovic, D. 2004, *La valutazione del marchio,* Milan: Egea.

Preston, R. 2000, 'Content is King', *New Media & Society,* 2(3): pp. 253–67.

Provenzo, E. 1991, *Video Kids: Making Sense of Nintendo*, Cambridge, MA: Harvard University Press.

Puro, J.P. 2002, ' Finland: A Mobile Culture', eds Katz, J.E. and Aakhus, M. *Perpetual Contact: Mobile Communication, Private Talk, Public Perform-ance*, Oxford: Oxford University Press.

Putnam, R. 2000, *Bowling Alone: The Collapse and Revival of American Community*, New York: Simon & Schuster.

Quart, A. 2003, *Branded: The Buying and Selling of Teenagers*, London: Arrow.

Radway, J. 1984 (1991), *Reading the Romance*, Durham, NC: University of North Carolina Press.

Rainwater, L., Coleman, R. and Handel G. 1959, *The Workingman's Wife: Her Personality, World and Life Style*, New York: Oceana.

Rajagopal, A. 1999, 'Thinking through Emerging Markets: Brand Logics and the Cultural Forms of Political Society in India', *Social Text*, 17(3).

Rathnell, J.M. 1964, 'Life Style Influences and Market Segmentation: An Introduction', ed. Greyser, S.A. *Toward Scientific Marketing*, Proceedings of the Winter Conference of the American Marketing Association, 27–28 December 1963, Boston, MA, Chicago, IL: American Marketing Association.

Redclift, M. 2004, 'Chewing Gum: Taste, Space and the "Shadow-lands"', paper presented at the conference *Consumption, Modernity and the West*, Pasadena, CA, 16–17 April.

Reeves, R. 1961, *Reality in Advertising*, New York: Knopf.

Regan, K. 2002, 'Epinions: An E-commerce Success that Almost Wasn't', *E-commerce Times*, 29 May.

Rehak, B. 2003 'Playing at Being: Psychoanalysis and the Avatar', eds Wolf, M.P. and Perron, B. *The Video Game Theory Reader*, New York: Routledge.

Reich, R.B. 1991, *The Work of Nations: Preparing Ourselves for the 21st Century*, New York: Knopf.

Rheingold, H. 1993, *The Virtual Community*, Reading: Addison-Wesley.

Rheingold, H. 2003, *Smart Mobs: The Next Social Revolution*, Cambridge, MA: Perseus Books.

Riewolt, O. 2002, *Brandscaping*, Basel: Birkhäuser.

Rifkin, J. 2000, *The Age of Access*, New York: Putnam.

Ritcher, M. 2002, 'New Billboards Sample Radios as Cars Go By', *The New York Times*, 27 December.

Ritchie, K. 1995, *Marketing to Generation X*, New York: Lexington Books.

Ritzer, G. 1999, *Enchanting a Disenchanted World: Revolutionizing the Means of Consumption*, Thousand Oaks, CA: Pine Forge Press.

Roche, D. 2000, *A History of Everyday Things*, Cambridge: Cambridge University Press.

Rodgers, A.L. 2002, 'Memo to Brands: Surrender', *Fast Company*, April.

Rose, N. 1999, *The Powers of Freedom*, Cambridge: Cambridge University Press.

Rutherford, P. 1994, *The New Icons? The Art of Television Advertising*, Toronto: University of Toronto Press.

Samuel, L.R. 2001, *Brought to You Buy: Postwar Television Advertising and the American Dream*, Austin, TX: University of Texas Press.

Sanjek, R. 1996, *Pennies from Heaven: The American Popular Music Business in the Twentieth Century*, Oxford: Oxford University Press.

Sassatelli, R. 2004, *Consumo, cultura e societa*, Bologna: il Mulino.

Scanlon, P. 1995, *Inarticulate Longings. The Ladies Home Journal: Gender and the Promise of Consumer Culture*, London: Routledge.

Scannell, P. 1996, *Radio, Television and Modern Life*, Oxford: Blackwell.

Schiller, D. 1999, *Digital Capitalism*, Cambridge, MA: MIT Press.

Schmitt, B.H. 1999, 'Experiential Marketing: How to Get Customers to SENSE, FEEL, THINK, ACT, RELATE to your Company and Brands', New York: The Free Press.

Schmitt, D. 2000, 'Creating and Managing Brand Experiences of the Internet', *Design Management Journal*, 11(4), pp. 53–8.

Schouten, J.W. and McAlexander, J.H. 1995, 'Subcultures of Consumption: An Ethnography of New Bikers', *Journal of Consumer Research*, 22: pp. 43–61.

Schrage, M. 1997, 'The Relationship Revolution: Understanding the Essence of the Digital Age', *The Merill Lynch Forum*, March.

Schudson, M. 1984, *Advertising: The Uneasy Persuasion*, New York: Basic Books.

Schultz, W. 2004, 'Reconstructing Mediatization as an Analytical Concept', *European Journal of Communication*, 19(1): pp. 87–101.

Schumpeter, P. 1942, *Capitalism, Socialism and Democracy*, New York: Harper.

Scott, W.D. 1903, *The Theory of Advertising: A Simple Exposition of the Principles of Psychology in their Relation to Successful Advertising*, Boston, MA: Small, Maynard & Co.

Seabrook, J. 2002, Interview, *The Merchants of Cool*, www.pbs.org/wgbh/pages/frontline/shows/cool/interviews/seabrook.htm, 12 September.

Seguela, J. 1982, *Hollywood lave plus blanc*, Paris: Flammarion.

Seth, J. 1970 'Multivariate Analysis in Marketing', *Journal of Advertising Research*, 10(1).

Sexton, R. 1995, 'The Origin of alt.sex' (http://www.vrx.net/usenet/history/alt.sex/).

Sherman, C. 2003, 'DealTime to Acquire Epinions', Searchenginewatch.com, 12 March.

Sherrington, M. 1995, 'Branding and Brand Management', ed. Baker, A.J. *Company Encyclopedia of Marketing*, London: Routledge.

Sherry, J. 1998, *Servicescapes: The Concept of Place in Contemporary Markets*, Lincolnwood, IL: NTC Publications.

Shields, R. 2003, *The Virtual*, London: Routledge.

Silberman, S. 1999, 'Just say Nokia', *Wired*, September.

Simmel, G. 1904 (1997), *Philosophie der Mode*, Berlin: Pan Verlag; trans. eds Frisby, D. and Featherstone, M. *Simmel on Culture*, London: Sage.

Sklair, L. 1991, *Sociology of the Global System*, Baltimore, MD: Johns Hopkins University Press.

Slater, D. 1998, 'Trading Sexpics on IRC: Embodiment and Authenticity on the Internet', *Body and Society*, 4(4): pp. 91–117.

Slater, D. 2002, 'Making Things Real: Ethics and Order on the Internet', *Theory, Culture and Society*, 19(5/6): pp. 227–45.

Smith, W.R. 1956, 'Product Differentiation and Market Segmentation as Alternative Marketing Strategies', *Journal of Marketing*, July.

Smythe, D. 1981, *Dependency Road: Communications, Capitalism, Consciousness and Canada*, Norwood, NJ: Ablex.

Sombart, W. 1967, *Luxury and Capitalism*, Ann Arbor, MI: University of Michigan Press.

Stalnaker, S. 2002, *Hub Culture: The Next Wave of Urban Consumers*, New York: Wiley.

Stansell, C. 1986, *City of Women: Sex and Class in New York, 1789–1860*, Chicago, IL: University of Chicago Press.

Sterling, C.H. and Kitross, J.M. 1990, *Stay Tuned: A Concise History of American Broadcasting*, Belmont, CA: Wadsworth.

Strathern, M. 1988, *The Gender of the Gift*, Berkeley, CA: University of California Press.

Swiencicki, M. 1999, 'Consuming Brotherhood: Men's Culture, Style and Recreation as Consumer Culture, 1880–1930', ed. Glickman, L. *Consumer Society in American History*, Ithaca, NY: Cornell University Press.

Talid, R. 2000, 'Malaysia: Power Shifts and the Matrix of Consumption', ed. Beng-Huat, L. *Consumption in Asia: Lifestyles and Identities*, London: Routledge.

Tapscott, D. 1996, *The Digital Economy*, New York: McGraw-Hill.

Tarde, G. 1901 (1989), *L'opinion et la foule*, Paris: Presses universitaires de la France.

Tarde, G. 1904, *Psychologie économique*, Paris.

Taylor, T.L. 2003, 'Whose Game is it Anyway? Negotiating Corporate Ownership in a Virtual World', unpublished paper, Department of Communication, North Carolina State University, Raleigh, NC.

Tedlow, R. 1990, *New and Improved: The Story of Mass Marketing in America*, New York: Basic Books.

Terdiman, D. 2004, 'No Will to Keep *Uru Live* Alive', *Wired News*, 13 February.

Terranova, T. 2004, *Network Cultures: Politics for the Information Age*, London: Pluto.

Thompson, C.J. and Troester, M. 2002, 'Consumer Value Systems in the Age of Postmodern Fragmentation: The Case of the Natural Health Microculture', *Journal of Consumer Research*, 28(4): pp. 550–71.

Thompson, E.P. 1968, *The Making of the British Working Class*, Harmondsworth: Penguin.

Todreas, T. 1999, *Value Creation and Branding in Televisions Digital Age*, Westport, CT: Quorum Books.

Townsend, A. 2002, 'Mobile Communications in the Twenty-first Century City', eds Brown, B., Green, N. and Harper, R., *Wireless World*, London: Springer.

Travis, D. 2000, *Emotional Branding: How Successful Brands Gain the Irrational Edge*, Roseville, CA: Prima Venture.

Turkle, S. 1996, *Life on the Screen: Identity in the Age of the Internet*, London: Weidenfeld & Nicolson.

Turow, J. 1997, *Breaking up America: Advertisers and the New Media World.* Chicago, IL: University of Chicago Press.

Twitchell, J. 1996, *Lead Us Not into Temptation: The Triumph of American Materialism*, New York: Columbia University Press.

Upshaw, L. 1995, *Building Brand Identity: A Strategy for Success in a Hostile Marketplace*, New York: John Wiley.

Urry, J. 2000, *Sociology Beyond Societies*, London: Routledge.

Urry, J. 2003, *Global Complexity*, Cambridge: Polity.

Van Ham, P. 2001, 'The Rise of the Brand State', *Foreign Affairs*, September/October.

van Impe, M. 2003, 'Nintendo sees Threat from Mobile Phones', Mobile CommerceNet (www.mobile.commerce.net), 9 January.

Vanderbildt, T. 1998, *The Sneaker Book*, New York: The New Press.

Veblen, T . 1899 (1994), *The Theory of the Leisure Class*, New York: Dover.

Virno, P. 1996, 'The Ambivalence of Disenchantment', eds Hardt, M. and Virno, P. *Radical Thought in Italy*, Minneapolis, MN: University of Minnesota Press.

Virno, P. 2002, *Grammatica della moltitudine*, Rome: DeriveApprodi.

Warner, W.L. 1949, *Social Class in America*, New York: Harper.

Wasko, J. 1994, *Hollywood in the Information Age*, Cambridge: Polity Press.

Wattanasuwan, K. 2002a, 'When White Elephants Came to the Capital: Negotiating the Self in the New Consumption Space', Working paper, Bangkok, Tammasat University.

Wattanasuwan, K. 2002b, 'The Young Noveau Riche and Luxury-brand Consumption', Working Paper, Bangkok, Tammasat University.

Weber, M. 1948, 'Politics as a Vocation', eds Gerth, H.H. and Mills, C.W. *From Max Weber: Essays in Sociology*, London: Routledge.

Weiss, M.J. 1989, *The Clustering of America*, New York: Harper & Row.

Wells, D.W. 1974, 'Foreword', ed. Wells, D.W. *Life Style and Psychographics*, Chicago, IL: American Marketing Association.

Wells, W. and Tigert, D. 1971, 'Activities, Interests and Opinions', *Journal of Advertising Research*, 11: pp. 27–35.

Wernick, A. 1991, *Promotional Culture*, London: Sage.

Whetten, D. and Godfrey, P. 1998, *Identity in Organizations*, London: Sage.

White, N. 2000, *Reconstructing Italian Fashion*, Oxford: Berg.

Whitty, M. and Carr, A. forthcoming, 'Cyberspace as Potential Space: Considering the Web as a Playground to Cyber Flirt' (forthcoming in *Human Relations*).

Whyte, W.H. 1955, 'The Consumer in the New Suburbia', ed. Clark, L.H. *Consumer Behaviour: The Dynamics of Consumer Reaction*, New York: New York University Press.

Whyte, W.H. 1956, *The Organization Man*, New York: Simon & Schuster.

Wild, K. and Scicluna, M. 1997, 'Accounting for Brands: The Practitioners' Perspective', ed. Perrier, R. *Brand Valuation*, London: Premier Books: pp. 87–115.

Wildt, M. 1998, 'Changes in Consumption as Social Practice: West Germany During the 1950s', eds Strasser, S., McGovern, C. and Judt, M. *Getting and Spending: European and American Consumer Societies in the Twentieth Century*, Cambridge: Cambridge University Press.

Williams, R. 1958, *Culture and Society, 1780–1950*, London: Chatto & Windus.

Williams R.H. 1982, *Dream Worlds: Mass Consumption in Late Nineteenth Century France*, Berkeley, CA: University of California Press.

Willis, P. 1990, *Common Culture: Symbolic Work at Play in the Everyday Cultures of the Young*, Milton Keynes: Open University Press.

Wittel, A. 1999, 'Towards a Network Sociality', *Theory, Culture & Society*, 18(6): pp. 51–76.

Wolf, M.J. 2001, *The Entertainment Economy: The Mega Media Forces that are Reshaping our Lives*, London: Penguin.

Wolf, M.P. 2001, 'The Video Game as Medium', ed. Wolf, M.P. *The Medium of the Video Game*, Austin, TX: University of Texas Press.

Worland, R. and Slayden, D. 2000, 'From Apocalypse to Appliances: Post-war Anxiety and Modern Convenience in "Forbidden Planet"', eds Dessor, D. and Jowett, G.S. *Hollywood Goes Shopping*, Minneapolis, MN: University of Minnesota Press.

Wright, S. 2002, *Storming Heaven: Class Composition and Struggle in Italian Autonomist Marxism*, London: Pluto.

Yankelovich, D. 1964, 'New Criteria for Market Segmentation', *Harvard Business Review*, Spring.

Ziff, R. 1974, 'The Role of Psychographics in the Development of Advertising Strategy and Copy', ed. Wells, D.W. *Life Style and Psychographics*, Chicago, IL: American Marketing Association.

Zizek, S. 1999, 'You May!', *London Review of Books*, 18 (March): pp. 3–6.

Zuboff, S. 1988, *In the Age of the Smart Machine*, London: Heineman.

Index